Praise for

CREAM
of the

"This book is new, exciting and different. It will help people improve their performance because they want to, not because they have to. I have worked with Louise and I've seen first hand that her ideas for accelerating improvement really work. *Cream of the Corp.* will help you tap into all the potential your people have—every day. I highly recommend it."

Larry Wilson
Acclaimed entrepreneur, facilitator and speaker
Founder of Wilson Learning Corporation and
Pecos River Learning Centers
Co-author of *Play to Win*

"*Cream of the Corp.* is an easy (and fun) read for managers who must find ways to creatively motivate individual employees, change their behaviors and improve performance."
Jerry McAdams
Author, *The Reward Plan Advantage* and *Rewarding Teams*

"*Cream of the Corp.* is a unique and outstanding book. Rarely does a business book provide such pragmatic advice on how to improve your business while at the same time being fun, dynamic and entertaining. This book can make a huge difference in how you run your business."
Kevin Cashman
CEO, LeaderSource
Best-selling author, *Leadership from the Inside Out*
and *Awakening the Leader Within*

CREAM
of the
CORP.

CREAM
of the

CORP.

An Ingenious Way to Get People Doing
Things that Accelerate Profits
NOW!

Louise S. Anderson, CEO

Anderson Performance Improvement Company
Hastings, Minnesota

Cream of the Corp.
*An Ingenious Way to Get People Doing
Things that Accelerate Profits NOW!*

Published by
Anderson Performance Improvement Company
12181 Margo Avenue South
Hastings, MN 55033-9437
www.andersonperformance.com

For information about our products and services, call 651-438-9825.

Credits
Chief humorist and bull monitor: Howard Anderson
Idea motivator: Kathleen Carter
Master orchestrator and timeline master: Carol Hadac
Illustrator and designer: Brad Norr, Brad Norr Design
Writer: N. Visible

Library of Congress Cataloging-in-Publication Data
ISBN: 0-9742525-0-6

Manufactured in the United States of America

{ For additional copies of ***Cream of the Corp.***, call 651-438-9825 }
{ or visit www. andersonperformance.com }

CONTENTS

1

OFF TO THE RACES

Are you tired of reading management stuff that sounds more like a textbook than a playbook?

So am I. That's why I meet monthly with a group of CEOs to talk about real-world problems, and solutions we can put to work NOW.

In fact, I've been meeting with CEOs of major companies for 23 years. I've been in their strategy sessions and their bull sessions. I've been kicked out of the boardroom, and then invited back in. Why? Because I've had the audacity to tell leaders that what they are doing will not *accelerate growth today*—and maybe not even next quarter.

Now stay with me. This book may feel like a swift kick in the pants, but it's only going to hurt for a little while.

I can show you how you can accelerate accomplishing your key strategies and earn 1,000 percent ROI on a $500K investment. (If you're curious, take a sneak preview and look at page 31.) And it's not by making people feel good about coming to work.

The secret lies in designing personal consequences that motivate lasting behavior change. This is the defining concept of performance improvement, and it isn't as simple as it may sound. This book simplifies concepts for you so you won't have to wade through a bunch of business jargon to get to the practical steps your company must take today to get results this quarter.

Cream of the Corp

If you're like most leaders, you may believe you've tried everything to get people to improve their performance. No wonder most executives are cynical about rewards. Typically, rewards are the most rewarding only for the superheroes who can achieve the stretch goals put before them—again and again. You know, your star performers, the muscle-bound athletes who can catch a speeding bullet in their teeth—typically the top 10 percent.

Then there are those who consistently drag across the finish line last, another 10 percent or so. Which leaves the Eighty Percent Club—those ordinary, everyday people who want to do a good job but either aren't inspired enough to finish with the leaders, or simply don't know how to deliver what's expected.

This book is about your middle performers. It's about helping your 80 percent group rise to a new level so they can join the cream of the corp. How do you do that? Please tell me "cash rewards" did not just flash across your brain.

I don't believe any amount of money can buy behavior change. Employees need a goal that means something to them personally. If they're going to invest the extra energy it takes to improve their performance, people should have a say in what their efforts will earn them. That's why *choice* is a much more effective motivator than cash.

The best way to give employees a choice is through an *e*Points system. This is a sophisticated, high-tech banking system that allows participants to earn points as they achieve their goals, and then spend their accrued points on items they really want. I'll explain in more depth later why *e*Points are superior to cash as a reward currency.

Now that we've talked about the basics of performance improvement, we're ready to think about the big "how" question:

How can you move more of your middle performers into your tier of top performers?

The short answer: First, you figure out exactly what your top performers are doing, and then you reward everyone who copies that behavior.

If this sounds like a no-brainer, you should hear some of the conversations I've had with corporate leaders.

These executives have watched incentive programs lose steam after the first lap around the track, and they've long since stopped cheering. Now they just dole out the rewards to their top performers (if you call cash a reward), viewing rewards as one more cost of doing business.

No one has ever demonstrated to them that the real goal of rewards is to motivate behavior change, *not* to thrill people with more trips, more merchandise or more money. The goal is to accelerate results.

That's right. Rewards, properly used, are a powerful tool for keeping people focused on the results you need *today* by reinforcing the behaviors and activities that get those results. The gains you achieve in the race make work more rewarding for *everyone*—especially you. But wait, I'm getting ahead of myself.

On Your Mark ...

Today's market is a horse of a different color. Sure, you probably thought the same thing a few years ago. But the race has intensified.

In case you hadn't noticed: We're in a global market that's precariously balanced on the edge of the future. Technology is no longer at the top of the boardroom's list of front-runners. Most of us are ISO-certified and have decent processes, so products are commoditized. We have to keep innovating to give oh-so-picky customers a better experience. And we have to do it with a leaner staff. In sum, we have ever-higher hurdles to clear.

We need results and we need them yesterday.

But let me tell you what I consistently hear from leaders at the highest levels in Fortune 500 companies. It goes something like this:

Me: Nice to meet you, _____ .

(Fill in your name here.)

After we get acquainted, I ask a question that resonates immediately with most leaders:

Me: If you could wave a magic wand and actually *get* the **one thing** you must do this year to be successful, what would that be? (Remember, this is a business book!)

Leader (without blinking): I need to (pick one or more):
A. Increase profits
B. Improve customer satisfaction
C. Increase speed to market
D. Improve quality
E. Increase sales
F. All of the above

Me: Tell me, how many of your people have to improve to meet your goals this year?

Leader: Everyone.

Me: So … do you have a plan to do something *radically* different?

Leader: Well, we're going to increase efficiencies, lower our manufacturing costs, improve quality, blah, blah, blah.

Me: In other words, you're planning to get better results by doing the same things you've been doing? Isn't that the well-worn definition of insanity?

Leader: You don't understand. My hands are tied. (Pick one or more):
A. We need management buy-in.
B. We need training.
C. If we had more money, we could do what we need to do.
D. Information Technology doesn't understand our business.
E. Marketing gets all the money.
F. We need more data.
G. The union won't let us do things differently.

Me: Want to know who's really to blame? *Every manager who isn't calling people to action.* (See the blank you filled in above— could it be you?)

Long story short: Are you on the right track? I recently met with the leaders of a major corporation whose main competitor had made front-page news by shading their financials. With the competition in disarray, I enthusiastically presented the client with ideas for taking the market by storm.

"Oh, no," they said. "We can't do that! There's too much change happening, too fast. We just worked around the clock to get ready for next year's strategic planning session. We can't change course now."

They're racing full-speed ahead, but they're still on last year's track.

Get Back in the (Right) Race

Don't worry. I'm going to help you figure out how to call your people to action. And I'll help you think about what will motivate them to make the changes that are critical to this year's success.

What I *won't* help you do in this book is formulate your strategy. You probably have more strategies than you know what to do with. I want to help you *accelerate* the deployment of your most important strategies. If you don't like the word deploy, think of it this way:

I will help you get things done—fast.

Before you start to get things done fast, I'll help you make sure you've targeted the right things (within your strategic plans) to get done. First and foremost, we have to agree on one thing: Change happens through *people.*

Most leaders know change comes primarily through people, process and technology. But when you think about it, people are the common denominator. *People* have to use the technology. *People* have to improve the processes. Yet I frequently hear leaders say, "We'll turn our attention to people after we finish getting this new software system up and running."

Not This ...   **But This**

Meanwhile, people keep doing the same things—and producing the same results. And the line item for new technology keeps growing and growing while revenues and profits keep shrinking.

That's why this book does not focus on process or technology. Its focus is people, and more specifically people's *behavior*. Getting people to behave in ways that will improve your company's bottom line.

To that cynical voice in your head: If behavior change sounds like manipulation, keep in mind that other people are influencing the behavior of your employees every day. Their phone companies reward them for talking more. The local coffee shop gives them free coffee when they keep mainlining there. Free airline miles entice them to take more trips on one airline so they can ... take more trips.

Wake up and smell the espresso. Why should your employees be talking on the phone more and drinking more java and jetting around when they could be working harder for you? Maybe it's time for you to borrow some ideas from your corner coffee shop. Maybe it's time for you to sell your ideas to your employees and get them engaged in what you really need to do.

Why You Need This Book

This book will show you how to use what you already have to get results in terms of behavior change. This is not a theory. I'll show you case studies of programs that have produced incremental margins ranging from 200 percent to nearly 1,500 percent. You'll see that this method works with blue-collar employees just as effectively as with the white-collar crowd, and in union and non-union environments. If you don't believe it, read on.

You'll learn how to identify your high performers and clone their behaviors to get faster results. Don't worry. This kind of cloning doesn't require any lab work. And it's not illegal, either.

What about cash as a motivator? You won't have to read much further to understand why, even though people say they love money, cash is not what it's cracked up to be. I'll show you how to create the most effective mix of resources for quick results *and* lasting behavior change.

You'll learn how to avoid paying for the results you would have gotten anyway, and instead pay only for incremental improvement.

I'll show you how to select criteria for successful behaviors and how to make those behaviors verifiable so you can avoid runaway reward budgets.

And—I knew you'd ask—I'll make sure you can measure whether the targets you set were actually hit. You'll be able to produce reports that not only *sound* intelligent and look pretty, but have something to do with whether you actually accomplished your goals. (Hint: That's ROI.)

In summary, this book will show you how to focus people's behaviors on what is really important. Why? Because talk is cheap. If people aren't taking *action* to achieve your strategies, you won't hit the results you need. Period.

What's up with the cows?

When you meet **Louise Anderson,** CEO of Anderson Performance Improvement Company (APIC), you'd never guess that she's spent considerable time hanging around with cows. She doesn't remind you in the least of anything connected with a barnyard. But she did grow up on a farm in the Midwest.

Louise was a national sales manager in New York City for Milliken & Company when she became intrigued with the performance improvement industry. She soon joined a major performance improvement firm as its first female account executive. In 1994, she returned to her Midwestern roots and started APIC, located in the charming river town of Hastings, Minnesota, just south of St. Paul.

From her agrarian background, Louise learned many lessons. "Never once did my dad yell at his kids, 'Pick more corn!'" she says. "He knew the preparation of the topsoil and the quality of the seed would determine the yield of the crop. Even more important was the fine art of doing the right things at the right time—not too early, not too late."

Louise's clients are mostly Fortune 500 companies, none agrarian, and she's found that the same principles she learned on the farm hold true in the most sophisticated corporation.

Today, Louise is one of the foremost experts on performance improvement. She has designed and implemented thousands of behavior-based programs for well-known corporations. She's regularly invited to speak on performance improvement and corporate growth. Oh, and when she's not helping other companies achieve record-breaking growth ... she keeps company with a few cows.

2

{ *Principle 1* }

START WITH WHAT YOU HAVE
AND KEEP IT SIMPLE

How can you as a leader possibly keep up with the frantic pace of change?

The answer is simple, but only if you keep it simple (and I plan to help you do that): Let people know what they have to do *today* to achieve your organization's goals.

I believe the best way to keep them on the right track—that is, the fast track—involves the use of well-designed reward and recognition programs. The challenge is that most reward programs don't resemble a racetrack. They seem more like a maze.

It's the same picture I started to paint in the first chapter: The top performers head single-mindedly down the path toward the goal—a pile of cash. At the end of the year, the ones who get the cash are a little richer and a little happier.

A few in the mass of middle performers, the Eighty Percent Club, try but don't make the cash. They go back to the starting line with the ones who don't even try, the low performers. Back to business as usual.

The vast majority of employees just want to tune out the hoopla about management's latest program so they can get their work done. They aren't even aware of the latest program's goal and *what,* specifically, they need to do to make a difference.

And what about the leader who's running the program? Maybe he's closer to accomplishing his main strategy. Maybe he isn't. Can he tell whether people's behavior is changing? Maybe, maybe not. His metrics have nothing to do with behaviors. Either way, the cash he's spending on rewards has his stomach churning, his head throbbing and his palms sweating.

The Role of Rewards and Recognition

Based on this typical scenario, you may be thinking reward programs are just one more flavor-of-the-month initiative—or at least it seems as if there's a new goal every month. The maze keeps changing so fast, everyone's confused.

Before we talk about reward programs, let's get a couple of things straight. First, a reward program is *not* a corporate strategy or a stand-alone initiative. An executive vice president at a bank told me recently, "I've got seven strategies. If I put another strategy like a reward program in place, people will be totally confused. They'll have eight strategies to achieve."

No, no, no. A reward program, correctly designed, will help you *accelerate* the accomplishment of your strategies by keeping people focused on the results you need *today.* A reward program is a *tactic,* something that helps you achieve your strategies. It's an accelerator.

Second, forget about the sweaty palm stuff. You don't have to hire a consultant. You don't have to train people to navigate a complicated maze. You don't even have to go out and buy new software (sorry, if that's your gig). Reward programs should not be an expense. They actually should be a self-funding investment.

Yes, I know consultants say that about myriad products. But you really *can* achieve ROI high enough to achieve significant gains *and* cover the costs of a program. Later, I'll show you where to find your cash cows. For now, suffice it to say, it's wise to target the most profitable areas of your organization and get some early wins.

The main point is that you must start with what you have and keep it simple.

Why Rewards Fail

When reward programs fail, as they sometimes do, it's often because of a complex mix of factors. I want to focus on three common factors: the wrong reward offered at the wrong time on the wrong metrics.

The wrong reward ... Many programs offer rewards that look suspiciously like compensation. After all, if it feels like money and smells like money, it must be ... an entitlement. Once you give extra money, taking it away feels like a cut in pay. Ouch. I'll go into more depth later about why cold cash is not such a hot idea.

... At the wrong time ... Most reward programs dole out rewards when the bottom-line results are in, typically at the end of the fiscal year. I call that rewarding on autopsy. Suppose the goal of your program is to increase customer retention. By the time the results are in, your customers could be dead. It's too late to do anything to correct course.

... On the wrong metrics. Instead of focusing on behaviors, results are expressed in terms of how your division or organization performed collectively. And your metrics probably don't tell you *why* your numbers are off.

Let's say the body count is staggering—you've lost a record number of loyal customers. You have no idea who killed (or wounded) the customer relationships. The only good news is that you saved money on rewards.

Or maybe you did retain a record number of customers. Which employees managed this incredible feat and how did they do it? You don't know. (Hmmm, are you starting to wonder about behaviors?)

So now you're rewarding *everyone* for the good work of a few. Can you repeat the results next year? Only if your mystery performers are still around. You might call this throwing money to the wind.

Long story short: Wrong reward, wrong time, wrong metrics. In order to fix its reward budget, one company bought six SUVs to give to top performers who increased sales after learning a complex new selling process. The SUVs would be rewarded when sales results were in at the end of the year (wrong time).

The problem was that the salespeople did not know exactly what they had to do to achieve the results (wrong metric), nor was the prospect of earning an SUV perceived as possible (wrong reward). The program's results paid for about half of the vehicles. Not one vehicle was given away.

How to Get Started

I promised I'd show you how to start with what you have. You have a strategy. You have paid employees. You will have incremental gains out of which to fund the program (trust me). Now you can get started. And I'll show you how you can keep it simple.

1. Link the Reward to Your Main Strategy

Well, duh, you may be thinking. Who wouldn't link the reward to their strategy? You may be surprised. As I tell my clients,

It's good to dream big strategic dreams!

But your big strategic dreams need to include *behaviors* that gain and sustain the *customer relationships* that make you *money.*

One company wanted its business-to-business sales force to close faster, increase margins and be more attentive to customers. Who wouldn't want those three things?

But you can't ask people to cross three goal lines at once, no matter how big the prize. The organization's *key* strategy was to increase the sales of a bundled solution (product *and* service), because their competitors would not be able to match the offer. So the firm offered *double* commissions on bundled sales and *no* commissions on sales of product alone.

They knew their key strategy, all right, but this was a breathtaking change for the sales force, which had been selling product and service separately for years. Not to mention that doubling commissions was like putting the cheese at the end of the maze without any rewards along the way to let them know they were on the right path.

Employees can smell a (dead) rat a mile away. These salespeople saw the whole design of the maze changing. They'd put a lot of time into product sales already in the funnel, and now the rules of the game were different and they could lose their commissions on the sales they'd already worked hard on but hadn't yet closed. Within a month, the company's top performers were seriously sniffing out other companies' mazes.

This company had based commission on its key strategy. But it hadn't figured out how to define that strategy in terms of the behaviors and activities that would get the fast results it needed to remain competitive in its marketplace. Which brings us to our next point.

2. Create a Clear Call to Action

Here's where many companies find it most challenging to keep it simple. I'll stay with the example of the bundling salespeople. The leaders knew their people were wandering away from the maze, so here's what they said:

"Not only will we double commissions, we will offer an all-expenses-paid trip to those who sell bundled solutions. We'll sweeten the pot!" Notice that they were focusing solely on their top performers, the ones who could perform the heroics needed to earn the higher rewards—the ones who were thinking about jumping ship.

They didn't realize their new maze design was faulty.

I asked them, "What do your salespeople—all of them, not just the top performers—need to do in order to sell product/service solutions to their customers?"

The answers came fast and furious: "They need knowledge! They need to profile their customers and spell out their needs to the support people back at the office! They need to collaborate with our engineers! They have to understand data better than they do today!"

That's when I gave them three rules for developing an effective Call to Action.

Rule Number One: Identify two behaviors/activities that are needed to get results.

Instead of rewarding those with the best vital signs at the end of the program, it's much better to reward on the behaviors you can observe along the way. I call them *early indicators.*

Now, please pay attention to this detail: For the sake of simplicity, when I say *behaviors,* I'm referring to *behaviors and/or activities*—anything someone has to do to get a result. I know this will annoy you strategist-types who happen to be reading this book, but try to relax and listen.

As I was saying, you need to reward people for the targeted behaviors called early indicators. It's as if you're taking the pulse, blood pressure and temperature of people's interest and engagement during the journey. You want to know people are still with you, not killing time in some obscure dead end while they dream of joining someone else's maze.

How do you do this? You select a couple of key behaviors, and you track them throughout the program so you can take corrective measures as needed. These are the behaviors that people must perform to achieve your strategies, the early indicators that answer the question: **What do I have to do first?**

Make it easy for people. Don't make them guess.

You may be thinking: Simple, my foot. You're saying to yourself, But you don't know our company. We have lots of technical jobs. We could never come up with just two behaviors to measure.

That's what a transportation firm believed. They had five job descriptions among the 350 people they wanted to reward. When they analyzed the jobs, though, they were able to identify the same four relevant behaviors. They focused on just two of those for a given job title.

Two Behaviors/Activities Per Job Title

Four Relevant Behaviors/Activites	Developer I	Developer II	System Admin.	Network Engineer I	Network Engineer II
	2 Early Indicators	2 Early Indicators	2 Early Indicators	2 Early Indicators	2 Early Indicators
1. Work Simplification			●		
2. Collaboration	●	●		●	●
3. Team Meeting Attendance				●	●
4. Knowledge Sharing/ Back-up Plan/ Code Review	●	●	●		

Rule Number Two: Identify one result metric.

Although the focus is on the early behaviors you need to get measurable results, you still have to have results indicators. In the example above, the result metric for all job descriptions was on-time delivery/percent uptime.

Why choose behavior and result metrics? It has to do with balancing metrics related to quality (behaviors) with those related to productivity (results). Most companies err on the side of productivity by measuring results almost exclusively.

But think about it. If you choose only quality indicators, productivity will suffer. If you choose only productivity measures, quality will suffer. See why you need balance?

Let me explain: In recent years, call center managers have realized that by rewarding reps for staying on the phone with customers to solve their problems (increasing quality), they have increased the average length of queue time (decreasing productivity). Customers have had to hold longer while reps were finding answers to questions or looking for products they could cross-sell. And we all know how fun it is to be put on hold for our entire lunch break.

Which brings us to rule number three.

Rule Number Three: Combine Rules Number One and Two.

In real life, things usually don't fit a one-two-three pattern. That's true here, too. But to avoid confusion (yours and mine), let's use this general guideline: We'll choose **two behaviors** and **one result metric** as goals for a reward program.

Typically—you'll notice this pattern throughout the book—at least one, and sometimes both, of the behaviors have to do with acquiring knowledge. This could be knowledge of a selling process, knowledge of products or technical knowledge. With today's technology, managers can easily verify people's knowledge by checking to see whether they've passed online quizzes.

Two behaviors and one result metric. This is the standard pattern I use, with variations, for most reward programs. Collectively, I call these metrics the *Call to Action*. I'll show you how to introduce your Call to Action in Chapter 3.

In the bundling sales example earlier in the chapter, the company chose to reward on this Call to Action:

Call to Action – Sales

- **Magic-wand wish:** Increase sales of multiple, bundled products and services (previous sales were product *or* service).
- **Behavior:** Ask open-ended questions (a consultative selling technique), as measured by management observation.
- **Behavior:** Know products, as verified by completion of quizzes.
- **Result:** Increase average revenue per call by levels ranging from 5% to 15%.

When the organization began using this Call to Action instead of rewarding with cash, solution sales (equipment bundled with service) increased by 26 percent. Prior to this program, the company had never achieved more than 9 percent improvement. **Of special note: In May and June, even though no incentive was in place, the *changed behaviors held.***

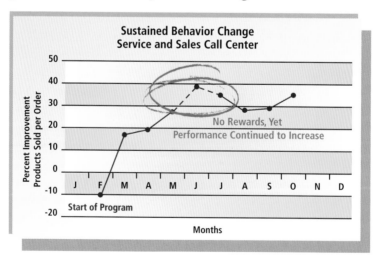

Here's a Call to Action that was designed for a call center that takes incoming customer calls.

Call to Action – Service

- **Magic-wand wish:** Reduce call-backs and improve customer satisfaction.
- **Behavior:** Know where to find the answers to customers' questions, as verified by completion of online quizzes.
- **Behavior:** Know products, as verified by completion of online quizzes.
- **Result:** Increase speed to resolution and reduce transfers.

How'd they do? The company was able to reduce call-backs by about 20 percent. The initial program not only reduced costs, but also achieved an ROI of more than 200 percent. As for customer satisfaction, the reduced call-back rate indicates that fewer customers needed to make repeated calls before resolving their issues.

Long story short: Try this at home. You can use behaviors and results to set up rewards for your kids. I have a friend who offered his son, Billy, $100 for every "A" Billy got on his report card. Billy was not impressed, and the continuing "Ds" on his report card reflected his lack of interest in an unreachable outcome.

My friend decided to try a different reward program, one based on the behaviors Billy needed in order to raise his grades. Here's the Call to Action he used:

Call to Action – Homework

- **Magic-wand wish:** Achieve all grades of C or higher.
- **Behavior:** Work in a quiet place for one hour each night five times per week, as verified by observation.
- **Behavior:** Do homework for 30 minutes four times per week, as verified by random checks. If homework is finished, read a book during that time.
- **Result:** Increase GPA by one point or better.

For each goal Billy met, he received points toward a 100-point go-cart. He had earned the go-cart before the final grades were in. Billy enjoyed the excitement of earning something he really wanted, and both father and son enjoyed the satisfaction of Billy's academic success as "As" appeared on his report card.

Don't Make People Search for a Sign

Think of it like this. When you make it clear to employees that they will be measured on key behaviors and results, and then make it easy for them to achieve those goals, it's like putting direction signs in the maze to mark the shortest path. When you reinforce them for achieving specific behaviors on their way to the goal, you're placing a tour guide at major intersections of the maze to assure them they're still on the right path.

People don't have to guess whether to turn right or left. They don't have to waste time at dead-ends. Why should it be harder than that?

3

{ *Principle 2* }

DRAMATIZE YOUR CALL TO ACTION

Now that you've marked the shortest path through the maze (those behaviors and results that will accomplish your strategic goals), how do you motivate people to go down that path?

You have to inspire them, give them a vision for doing their jobs better and arm them with the resources they need to succeed. Sound daunting? It isn't really. It all begins with the Call to Action.

Make Sure You *Have* a Clear Call to Action

Imagine what would happen if a movie director showed up the first day on location and mumbled some vague instructions to the cast and crew? Or, worse, what would happen if the director sent in a B actor to inspire the cast. Either way, it's unlikely the production would be a box-office hit.

Yet these are the scenarios I see again and again in corporations. The actors (employees) are told they must put on a good show, but they aren't given clear coaching on how to *deliver* a good show. Or the director (the top-level manager) delegates to middle managers the challenging task of inspiring the cast and laying down the ground rules.

When the cast realizes the director is less than enthusiastic about the project, most of the members go on strike, mentally if not physically.

To avoid these deflating scenarios, a good director gathers the cast and issues a strong Call to Action. The Call to Action is framed in the context of the company's key business strategies so that the cast of thousands (or hundreds or tens) understands how the current program fits into the bigger picture.

The director searches through his or her toolbox of dramatic techniques—imagination, creativity, drama, playfulness, humor (oh yes, and food)—and selects the right media to introduce the Call to Action in a way that is fun and memorable. This is usually done in the context of a high-energy launch event, during which the actors get inspired to reach deep inside and play their roles with all the talent they can muster.

Stage an Event with Emotional Appeal

If you were planning any major event, you'd think first about the invitation and/or the publicity. Then you'd work hard on items such as the set, sound and light, the program or script, the choreography and the memorabilia. A launch event is similar.

Funny thing, though, lots of people forget about the *audience*. If you're going to inspire your participants to higher performance, you have to appeal to their emotions, their desires, their dreams. The main point here is to make it personal—you know, the old WIIFM, What's in it for me? Here are a few pointers:

Throw a party. This isn't just any party. It's a unique event with its own character and it should be different from anything employees have ever experienced.

The context of this celebration can be as simple as a coffee break or as elaborate as a national sales meeting. Regardless of the venue, you'll want to:

- Ask a top-level manager to emcee, with enthusiasm and, if possible, with humor.
- Come up with a creative theme that is relevant to your participants. You're only as limited as your imagination. You'd be surprised what you can do, even on a limited budget. Two banks that had just merged used a Winning Combination theme, represented by the enduring symbol of Egyptian pyramids. Another company used a SuperTech theme for a program targeting technicians. A superhero cartoon mascot made the program playful and fun.
- Speak the language of the employees. If they think in terms of service, don't try to inspire them in "salesese."
- Pay attention to the participants' work culture (or lack thereof). If you're planning an event for the sales force, you may want to stage a frat party. Some people will do anything for free drinks. (Just wanted to see if you're still with me.)
- Use show and tell. In the "Long story short" on page 28, high performers came to the party and role-played their techniques for getting appointments with high-level clients. The effect was gripping. People could see that the Call to Action was really doable.

Clearly Communicate the Call to Action

If you read Chapter 2, you know that the Call to Action consists of 1) the behaviors and 2) the results that are critical to this year's success. "Sell more" is not a good Call to Action.

For the sake of simplicity, I am using the framework of two qualitative behaviors and one quantitative result. It usually is not this tidy, but this is a good starting place for defining your Call to Action.

Long story short: Set the stage. Sixty widespread branches of a telecommunications division that sells to large companies (enterprise sales) launched their program the same day during breakfast or lunch meetings.

The theme of the event was "Go for the Gold," which played off the upcoming Olympics. The company also emphasized the golden rewards that participants, enterprise-sales and engineering professionals, could earn.

The launch party was highly participative, and people who contributed ideas or best practices were awarded scratch-off cards with varying values, which could be redeemed for appealing merchandise on the program's Web site. Their Call to Action:

Call to Action – Sales
- **Magic-wand wish:** Increase sales of technologically advanced products by 8 percent.
- **Behavior:** Schedule a client appointment with a director-level manager or higher, as verified by manager ride-along.
- **Behavior:** Fill out a high-quality profile on the client, as verified by manager.
- **Result:** Close a sale to the targeted client.

The launch party was highly visual and hands-on. Salespeople learned:

• How to use the tools they already had. Enterprise-account managers demonstrated how to use the company's Web-based CRM system to access knowledge, create profiles and plan advanced solution sales.

• How to get appointments with upper-level managers. High performers role-played setting up meetings with C players—CEOs, CFOs, COOs. The actors dramatized conducting the needs analysis and partnering strategically, which are critical to successful sales appointments.

• How the program worked. Managers provided coaching, demonstrating how customer profiles would be verified. They also showed how to bank reward points.

Participants tracked their own and their peers' progress against the program's Call to Action, copying best practices along the way. Look at the immediate lift after the launch!

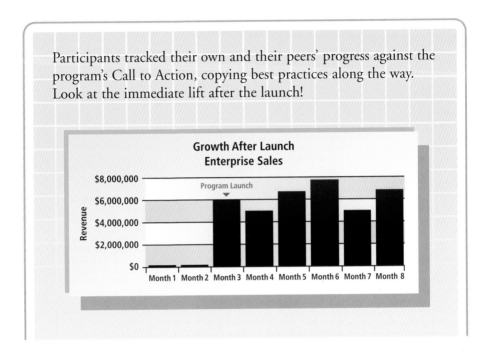

Clearly communicate the consequences. The consequences of achieving—and not achieving—the Call to Action are far-reaching, and cast members should understand that their individual performance has a significant impact on the company's strategic goals.

Of course, the only way to enforce the consequences is to *inspect* what you *expect*. You, the director, have to be constantly "tuned in" to observe whether each individual is performing his or her role to the standards you've directed.

Emphasize the consequence that matters most to the cast: People who achieve the behaviors and/or the results will receive rewards while those who don't, receive nothing. Everyone should be able to grasp in five minutes or less how they will be rewarded for achieving their goals.

In traditional programs, most participants—even those whose improvement is remarkable—receive nothing, because only a select few can hit the end-of-program goal. It's much more motivating when people know they'll be rewarded for their efforts, even if they don't win an Oscar for their performance.

Can you imagine engaging and calling ALL of your employees to action in support of your strategies NOW?

Keep marketing. Many companies let the message drop into oblivion after the launch. Here's where you'll want to pull out the creative stops with frequent communications to everyone whose role is critical to achieving the goals. Take advantage of every opportunity to broadcast the program's goals and the results-to-date by integrating Web-based communications, e-mails, posters and symbolic objects.

Don't forget to be enthusiastic. This is not a dress rehearsal. It's the real thing.

Long story short: Know it, then do it. A customer service call center kicked off its reward program with the theme "Together Better than Ever." The objectives of the program were to increase sales, which were flat, and improve customer service.

Call to Action - Service

- **Magic-wand wish:** Increase sales of products combined with services.
- **Behavior:** Know the products, as validated by completion of automated quizzes.
- **Behavior:** Use your knowledge on your calls, as validated by manager's observation.
- **Result:** Increase the number of multiple-product sales.

The message was first delivered at a festive meeting involving the entire call center. There were balloons, banners and buttons. Snack foods were served that taste better together than separate (e.g., salsa and chips), in keeping with the theme. A top manager got all excited about the goals of the program.

As the employees went back to work, colorful posters around the call center reminded them of their Call to Action. Managers immediately began to catch people doing things *right*, and reinforced them by giving them points the employees could spend for merchandise rewards. If employees needed to improve, they received on-the-spot coaching.

The graph below shows how quickly this program got results. **Revenue improved by more than 50 percent during the first month and was sustained for a program ROI of 1,042%!**[1]

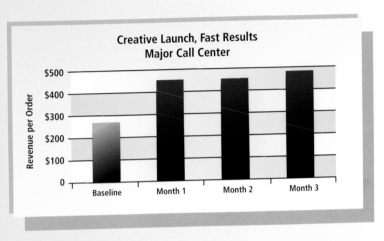

Creative Launch, Fast Results
Major Call Center

Use *e*Points to Reward Performance

As I mentioned in Chapter 1, using award credits, or *e*Points, in lieu of cash as a reward medium gets results faster. The *"e"* stands for electronic or excellence, depending on whom you ask. The value of an *e*Point is flexible; most companies set it between $.005 and $1.00.

A point system allows you to reinforce behaviors weekly or even daily with small rewards, giving out, say, 10 points at a time, without calling to mind a cash value. Cost savings over cash in tax liability and administrative labor make points particularly attractive.

Points also let you fit the requirement of the reward by offering a reward value commensurate with the effort required to earn it, i.e., a $50 reward for $50 of effort.

Participants can accrue *e*Points and spend them on items they've selected in a print or online catalog. They don't have the hassle of going out shopping, and they don't have to take time off work to travel. The trophy value of a tangible reward is that the employee and his or her family can enjoy the item for years to come, as a symbol of the hard work it took to earn the reward.

The average annual incentive-plan payout of $833 per employee[2] translates to about $55 per month after taxes.[3]

Which sounds more appealing: $55 per month toward your monthly phone bill for a year, or the latest electronics for your home entertainment system?

You may be asking: What about cast members who can't keep up? I've observed that when you're asking for change in an environment where people work together closely, such as a call center or a dealership, team dynamics often ease the need for a directive director. People compare notes on their progress and encourage those who are struggling to help them meet the goals.

The process tends to be self-correcting. Those who can't perform the required behaviors realize they are holding up the entire production. Typically, they take initiative to look for a different position that is a better fit for their skills.

The Show Must Go On!

Every production has a curtain time. As you can tell, lots of work must happen behind the scenes to meet that deadline. The more energy you put into making certain that people understand and can perform your Call to Action, the more rewarding your program will be. So, break a leg (as the expression goes), and get ready for a standing ovation.

Next I'll show you how to use rewards to speed up the rate of change.

Notes

[1] ROI Equation: $\dfrac{\text{Incremental margin} - \text{Cost of program}}{\text{Cost of program}} = \text{ROI}$

[2] Jerry L. McAdams, *The Reward Plan Advantage,* (San Francisco: Jossey-Bass Inc., Publishers, 1996), 256.

[3] Ibid.

4

{ *Principle 3* }

PLAY THE GAME
JUST LONG ENOUGH TO WIN

One thing that makes a traditional reward program such an amazing journey is that, in most companies, the journey lasts a long, long time. Once a reward is offered, managers think they have to leave it in place until… well, until the cows come home.

If a reward program is ended, managers reason, employees will be de-motivated because they will perceive (correctly) that they are making less without the program than they did with it—especially if the reward is cash. Think entitlement.

Companies would do much better to treat reward programs like football games. See the game clock running relentlessly in the background? That's the fiscal year. Hear that ugly buzzing sound every quarter? Better get hustling.

As a Rule, Keep Programs Short

My guideline: Run a program no longer than 60 days past the time it takes to achieve the behavior.

Even avid fans wouldn't watch an endless football game. It would become meaningless and boring. Same with rewards. Once players have achieved their goals, let them do their dance in the end zone. Then take a hiatus and get ready for the next game!

Practically speaking, this means running programs of varying lengths. Most programs should last about 60 days past the time it takes to achieve the two behavioral goals. That's the great thing about defining your goals in terms of behaviors, not end results. You can reward a salesperson for learning a new product or conducting a strategic meeting with a top-level decision maker (moving the ball down the field), a lot faster than you can reward her for closing a sale (making a touchdown), especially if the usual selling cycle is a year or more.

You may be asking: Who wants to play a game when the rules keep changing? This is a typical question, particularly from companies who are accustomed to leaving reward programs in place for a year or more. It seems counterintuitive to pull or change a program when it is still getting some results.

But it isn't the rules you need to change, only the plays. And why not create a sense of urgency and priority by rewarding a specific play for a limited time? Then participants know there's no time to lose in learning the new behaviors.

How do you avoid creating a flavor-of-the-month culture? You don't pull the platform of the program. You simply use a new baseline or focus on another critical activity to achieve continuous improvement. Run the program just long enough to get a lift, usually when about 60% to 80% of the participants have reached the goal.

Reinforce Knowledge Sharing

A telecommunication company wasn't convinced of the wisdom of a short program, but the managers agreed to try it. They used the best practices of their top performers to define their Call to Action:

Magic-wand wish: Increase revenue per call an additional 10% by adding a team goal to a program already in place.

Behavior: Share your own best practices with your partner location in teleconferences, as verified by management participation.
(The program was based on pairing high-performing locations with low-performing ones.)

Behavior: Deploy best practices. Report results in the next week's conference call, as verified by management participation.

Result: Increase team (two-location) revenue per call to earn a special tier of rewards over the platform program.

(**Note:** This Call to Action transformed a program that was originally based on *competition* between locations into one based on teaming up high- and low-performing offices in order to spread best practices.)

The company ran this program for 60 days as an overlay to its basic program. To earn a reward, teams had to improve 5 percent over baseline. During the first heat, 100 percent of the teams improved, even though they did not improve enough to earn a reward. As the program progressed, managers looked at the best practices of their new top-performing group and used those as target behaviors for another program.

Teams of high and low performers were rewarded for joint improvement of 10 percent or greater. After each heat, the goal was increased by 5 percent for another 60-day program. Low performers were excited to join a winning team, and the revenue per call achieved by the teams skyrocketed.

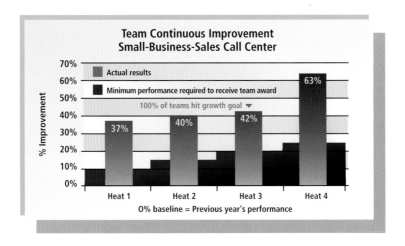

By the time the company ran the fourth heat of the program, managers were ecstatic. "We've broken the code," they said. By the third heat, 100 percent of the teams were hitting their growth goal.

Before the first heat, managers had been skeptical about achieving a goal of 19 percent overall improvement. In the end, though, the overall improvement was 42 percent over the previous year.

Keep Raising the Bar Carefully—No Pain, No Gain

A good coach thinks of today's game in the context of the entire season. He or she wants to keep the team's performance continuously improving from week to week. In business, however, managers often leave a stand-alone contest in place, missing opportunities to capture the time advantage of new and improved plays.

What's the difference between a stand-alone contest and continuous improvement?

Stand-alone contest. Most companies think they can improve performance by putting a reward on total sales. **(Remember the autopsy?)** The top few players—the winners—make their goal and get to bask their weary bodies in the sun for a few days. They become an elite sub-team. The rest of the team—the losers—stay home, knowing they have little hope of ever joining the sub-team.

Continuous improvement. When players work out consistently, they get stronger. The coach raises the bar and they try new things. He raises it again, and they adjust. A good coach rewards people for the pain of change. When everyone's running as fast as he can, the coach may turn his attention to passing, creating new pain. The season doesn't last forever, so there's no time to lose. Those who change first, gain most.

Continuous improvement should always be the intended result of your reward programs. Not only does the organization benefit; most employees are also happier at their job when they are learning and growing.

The key is that you can't continue to improve unless everyone hits certain minimums.

In football, players get four tries to carry the ball 10 yards. If they don't make that minimum, their team loses possession of the ball and they may find themselves at a big disadvantage when they should be capitalizing on an opportunity.

The key to rewards is to think in terms of downs, 10 yards at a time. Don't ask your players to run 100 yards on one play. The goal is too intimidating.

How to Keep the Game Moving

Your competitors have the same basic goals you have: to get new products to market fast; to find and keep customers; and to collect money faster. It's an intense game. You have very little time to determine the right play, issue a clear Call to Action and execute the play. The key is to know the right things to do, and to do them at top speed. Here's a framework for creating new plays and keeping the game moving:

First, identify your top performers.

Everyone knows who they are—the ones who are closing the most sales; getting commitments that put the check in the mail; fixing people's problems in short order and moving on to the next call.

Second, find out how those top performers are doing what they're doing.

You can do this by asking a series of intelligent questions:
- How's it going?
- What's contributing to your success?
- What are your obstacles?
- Hmmm. Any other obstacles?
- If you had a magic wand (I like magic-wand questions) and could add, change or delete anything today, what would it be?

The amazing thing is, people will answer these questions and you will learn their secrets of success. **Now that's using what you've got!**

Third, define what you need in terms of *behaviors* and *results*.

Is this beginning to sound like a cheer? It's the most important cheer you can learn. Find the two or three behaviors that your top performers are already doing to get the results you're looking for. If you're thinking *early indicators,* you've been paying attention.

As we learned in Chapter 2, we need to choose two behaviors (quality indicators) and one result metric (productivity indicator).

If we were building a winning football team, this means our focus would be on far more than just counting touchdowns. We understand that individual skills win games. Therefore, we would observe the quarterback for how he calls the plays and performs under pressure (behaviors) and count the number of yards completed (results). These are goals that everyone can improve on, and that are likely to lead to touchdowns.

In sales, we do NOT reward people simply for sales made. They're already receiving commission for that. Instead, we reward them for targeting 10 key clients and for going after the knowledge they need (behaviors). We validate that knowledge by observing how quickly they master their online quizzes. (Notice that we are not equating knowledge with training, since knowledge is training *applied*.) Then we reward them for closing targeted sales (results).

Long story short: What to say at half time. When managers are first introduced to the concept of early indicators, they are often at a loss for what to talk about in the locker room—you know, when they pull all their salespeople together for the weekly pep talk.

It took some time for a sales VP at a textile manufacturer to make the transition. Even though he had given a strong Call to Action, in weekly conference calls he kept asking the same old question: What did you sell last week?

Finally, he listened to feedback from the few reps who were achieving the Call to Action goals. These reps were only selling the targeted accounts, which sometimes took months (duh—it was a complex selling process!). They complained that since they didn't receive any recognition during weekly conference calls, they usually tried to avoid the calls by scheduling customer appointments.

The VP, embarrassed, began recognizing people for achieving the behaviors he had defined as critical: scheduling appointments with executives at targeted hospitality clients; and taking prospects to visit satisfied customers. As the VP recognized and reinforced these behaviors, performance improved and sales climbed dramatically.

Fourth, reward people on the spot for achieving the behaviors.

This is not as easy as it may sound. As I mentioned in Chapter 3, managers have to be on the ball to observe, evaluate and reinforce the new behaviors. They have to be consistent, rewarding only behaviors that meet the stated criteria.

When the success of the participants depends on the manager's role, you may want to establish a Call to Action for managers and reward them for their performance so their extra work does not go unnoticed (see Chapter 6).

How do managers reinforce good performance? You may think *e*Points sounds like a simple concept, but they are similar to a banking system—something that requires considerable know-how to put together. I've found *e*Points the most effective way to reward people on the spot for achieving goals. With the click of a mouse, a manager can give anyone reward points, which can be spent immediately or applied to the desired reward. People's excitement grows as their *e*Point balance grows.

Finally, clone your top performers' behaviors.

Don't wait until the end of the program to copy what high performers are doing. This is where you can gain speed over your competitors. Keep learning and applying best practices throughout the program to accelerate achieving your Call to Action goals. Then take a break and make a new plan. When you launch your next focus, set the baseline higher so you're not paying for achieving the same goals all over again.

This is where touchdowns are scored, because every percentage point you can move your middle 80 percent of performers, especially in a large company, can mean significant gains in incremental margin (see diagram on next page).

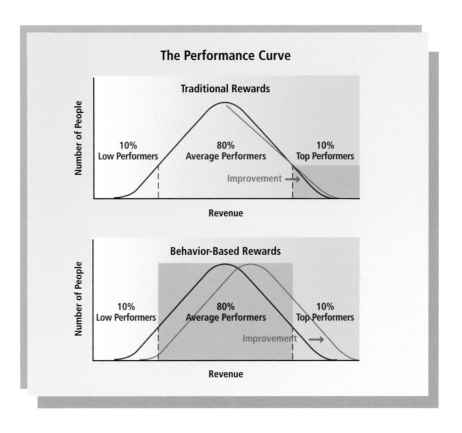

How do you help others copy what top performers are doing? It's much like the process I described above, which you used with the top performers at the beginning of the program:

- Identify your early adapters—the top performers who have unique ways of achieving the Call to Action goals.
- Go talk to a few of them.
- Ask them the intelligent questions until you figure out what each person did that worked—their best practices.
- Talk up what they are doing and reward and recognize others who take the same steps.
- Also reward those in their sphere of influence (managers, peers and/or support people identified as part of the best-practice process).

It's that simple. But the key is to do it *fast.*

Speed is Money

You're in the huddle. You, the coach, have 30 seconds to call the play and snap the ball. If you stay in the huddle too long, you'll be penalized.

Now the question is this: Will you leave an old reward program in place when the marketplace is intercepting your plays and throwing new demands at your team every day? Or will you keep raising the bar for higher levels of performance?

5

{ *Principle 4* }

MAXIMIZE THE MIX:
COMPENSATION, RECOGNITION AND REWARDS

We've already discussed the biggest obstacle to using rewards effectively, which is *time*—running a program (traditionally a contest) beyond its usefulness. In this chapter, I'll give you some clues for avoiding the other most common mistake companies make with rewards. It has to do with the mix of compensation, recognition and rewards.

A winning team is always considering how to improve performance. The coach's reputation rides on getting players to run faster, pass farther and hit harder so they can beat the competition.

Likewise in business, managers are always trying to find the magic elixir that will move their team toward optimal performance. The usual suspect is cash. Managers and employees alike believe that cash has mysterious motivational powers, although studies show that isn't necessarily so.

First, let's go to the scene of the crime: most companies.

> **Cash: The substandard motivator.** In a Watson Wyatt Worldwide study, almost a third of the nearly 700 companies surveyed said that merit pay does little to "encourage good performance." A full 95% of the respondents said their employees think of the extra cash as an entitlement.[1]
>
> In contrast, a research project conducted by the American Compensation Association that polled 1,600 companies found that non-cash rewards deliver a 3 to 1 return on investment over cash.[2]

Who moved the compensation?

That's the question you, the manager, may be asking if you're fairly new to the job and your team's comp packages seem out of sight. Here's the typical scenario: To get a sales team to reach new sales or revenue levels, *someone* offered them cash. The next year the cash pot had to be larger, the following year even larger, and so forth. (This is a sure formula for layoffs.)

Hmmm. Whodunit? It really doesn't matter whether your predecessor (or you!) made the decision, or whether it was made in the lunchroom or your office. Who cares whether the cash was committed in the form of stock options, paycheck bonuses or debit cards? It still smells suspiciously like compensation.

The problem is that people get used to having extra cash.

If you earned a $100 reward today, and were asked six—or even three— months from now what you did with it, chances are you wouldn't have a clue.

A study conducted by Wirthlin Worldwide showed that 47 percent of recipients either used their cash rewards to pay the bills or didn't remember what they used it for.[3]

Forty-seven percent. Doesn't that boggle your mind? If you're spending a million dollars on cash rewards, doesn't that mean you don't get any lasting benefit from $470,000? Nearly half!

The main problem with cash is that once it's taken away, it feels like a cut in pay.

I define compensation as the base salary, perks and benefits that attracted the person to the job in the first place. Which brings us to the special conundrum around rewarding *salespeople* with cash. They are already rewarded with cash in the form of commissions. So if cash were motivating, wouldn't they be motivated to sell more products and services in order to earn more commission?

Well, you're thinking, the top performers are. But the others? Guess not.

So how *should* people be rewarded? I was hoping you'd ask.

Food for Success

A good farmer will tell you: The secret is in the mix. You know what'll happen if you feed your valuable livestock a steady diet of junk food. (Hint: It's similar to what happens to you when you eat the same diet.)

If you want to get your cows to market quickly and in premium condition, you feed them a mix of corn, silage (hay) and protein. A mix is not as expensive as feeding them straight corn, and it gets you to market faster. Ideally, you'll want the high-performance mix that balances the corn with hay and minerals so you can optimize performance at the absolute minimum cost.

Likewise, you'll need the right mix of three items for successful employees:

Cash. Compensation is the corn of the market. It's your mainstay, the largest volume of the three and your biggest expense. You undoubtedly know the salary level your company must offer to attract and retain qualified employees without driving up overhead, as compared with your competitors. I'll assume that's what you're paying.

Recognition. Recognition is the tasty protein you sprinkle on top to keep your cows coming back to feed. Your company's unique ways of saying "Thank you." and "You are doing a great job!" comprise one form of recognition. The other form, which is discussed in this book, is the extra attention, prestige and rewards you offer your top performers.

Rewards. Rewards are the hay that helps you get higher performance from your investment in corn (compensation) and protein (recognition). Hay is the roughage that keeps the system, to put it delicately ... running smoothly. Farmers are constantly looking for just the right mix of corn, hay and protein to move performance to a higher level.

During my two-plus decades of experience with building reward programs, the well-known industry recommendation for an optimum mix has proved a good general guideline:

Cash: 88-93 percent of annual compensation package
Rewards: 5-8 percent of annual compensation package
Recognition: 2-4 percent of annual compensation package

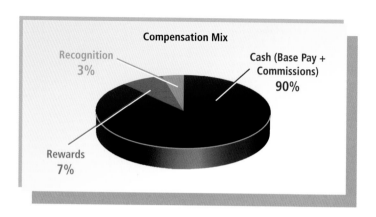

Compensation Mix

Recognition 3%

Cash (Base Pay + Commissions) 90%

Rewards 7%

Let's see how this works out practically. A salesperson who makes $100,000 is paid $90,000 in base pay and commissions and earns about $7,000 in non-cash rewards and $3,000 in recognition in the form of travel and other perks. A call center rep who earns $25,000 should receive $22,500 in salary, $1,750 in rewards and $750 in recognition.

Now, these funds will not be disbursed evenly because all employees do not perform evenly. The mix will also depend on the person's function.

The key is to pay your people within the industry average—or higher, to retain them longer. Then help them focus on the behaviors that will increase bottom-line results. How do you do this? You reward improvement and recognize results. Is this beginning to sound familiar?

Shift the Paradigm

Typically, an organization puts all of its levers—compensation, recognition and rewards—on the end result: higher levels of customer satisfaction, performance over quota, first-call resolution. It is surprising how often rewards are structured in a way that participants can make the maximum rewards and recognition without producing increased revenue for the company. In other words, companies are paying millions of dollars this year just to get the same results they got last year!

Traditional Rewards

RESULTS

Recognition

Rewards

Compensation

Under the new paradigm, you put rewards on the early behaviors (the ones that yield results) in addition to the improved result you identified in your Call to Action. Now you have a chance to shape behaviors long before you discover that you've lost customers and sales. In other words, you can get people doing things that accelerate profits NOW.

Behavior-Based Rewards

Why Non-Cash Rewards?

When it comes to rewards, managers think that what employees want is more money. Who wouldn't want more money? Employees themselves believe they want more money. But that doesn't necessarily prove that money is the best motivator.

My consistent observation over the years is that *choice* is a better motivator than money. With a non-cash reward system based on *e*Points, people get to choose what they want from a collection of high-quality items selected with their interests in mind. It's a guilt-free "purchase," and one with no specific monetary value attached for easy price comparison.

Please note: I am not talking about offering merchandise at inflated values your employees will immediately compute as ridiculous. One thing that sometimes gives non-cash reward programs a bad name is companies that offer $20 toasters for $80 worth of reward points. While most performance improvement companies figure some administrative costs into the cost of rewards, there's no need for obscene mark-ups.

Your HR department may tell you cash rewards are easier to track for tax purposes. But non-cash rewards actually have tax *advantages,* which means your reward dollars go further. You'll pay 100 percent of the tax on cash rewards, gift certificates and debit cards, but only 70 percent to 80 percent of the tax on merchandise value.[4]

The chart below summarizes the other advantages of non-cash rewards.

Why Non-Cash Rewards?

Dimension	Cash	Non-Cash
Compensation Comparison	Cash can be easily absorbed into personal budget; seems like a cut when it disappears.	Participants understand that the program will end; the opportunity is offered for a limited time only. They must act now.
Trophy Value (Memorability)	People usually don't display cash awards. Sometimes, they don't even remember what they bought with their cash.	Any tangible reward can serve as a reminder of the accomplishment that earned it.
Guilt Factor	Many feel cash should go toward paying the bills instead of toward a luxury item.	A tangible reward is a guilt-free "gift."
Perceived Value	$50 in cash is perceived as an amount that doesn't go very far.	A $50 item is often perceived as more valuable.
Motivation Factor	Cash, except for large amounts, is not exciting to promote.	A choice of tangible items can be advertised and marketed.
Token Economy (Points Banked as Rewards)	Cash is often perceived as entitlement.	Points are easy to bank, transfer and redeem.
Personal Goal Setting	With cash, management sets the reward amount as the goal.	Individuals can choose a reward they really want, and go for it.
Family/Friend Engagement	Family and friends have limited involvement in a cash program.	Family and friends can share in the excitement of the goal.
Tax Liability	Employer is taxed at higher rate on cash.	Tax liability is offset by other tax-related benefits.

Rule Out the Usual Suspect

Whenever companies want to increase revenue, the first idea out of the leader's mouth is consistently, "Let's increase compensation to the salespeople." Or, for a nonsales audience, "Let's offer a cash reward."

I suggest you ask yourself three questions before you decide to do that:

1. Are you putting your money on the right behaviors?

Companies often err in putting additional dollars on products sold rather than rewarding the behaviors required in order to capture those sales.

For example, I worked with a heavy equipment manufacturer that was in deep trouble after putting a hefty commission increase on the sale of a particular vehicle. The reps earned more for selling that piece of equipment, all right. Their commissions went up because of the big bonus. But on further investigation, we discovered that overall sales went down. Oops.

In another example, a call center client had posted five-dollar bills on the bulletin board. Reps could take one every time they sold a particular product. Try this if you ever want to spend $90,000 at the speed of light.

The flurry of individual sales created a lot of excitement among call reps. But we discovered that many of the customers who bought the product did not understand *why* they needed it. It took the company months to realize that the campaign had actually resulted in a *reduction* in revenue per call of more than 10 percent! For the Call to Action that solved this problem, see page 52.

2. Can you afford to keep paying out the cash indefinitely?

Does the word *entitlement* ring a bell? Once people get used to higher commissions, it's nearly impossible to take them away without losing your top performers. (Remember, when you take the cash away, it feels like a cut in pay.)

In the call center story above, when the five-dollar bills produced no improvement in revenue, managers got smart and started coaching the reps to ask open-ended questions so they could cross-sell products that really met customers' needs: "Who in your family uses the phone? Tell me about the kinds of things you use your phone for. How often do you compete with your kids for phone time?"

Let's look at this case in the terms we've been talking about:[5]

Call to Action - Sales

- **Magic-wand wish:** Increase sales by any amount (sales had been flat) while increasing customer satisfaction. (They'd been stung by the five-dollar-bill cash reward program—see page 51).
- **Behavior:** Ask specific open-ended questions, as verified by manager's observation.
- **Behavior:** Engage the customer (specific techniques were coached), as verified by manager's observation.
- **Results:** Increase revenue per call by levels ranging from 5% to 15%.

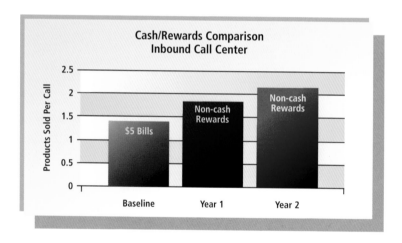

The outcome? The center's revenue per call grew 15 percent in a 90-day period! Until this time, the center had not experienced double-digit growth for as long as anyone could remember.

3. Are you rewarding the right people?

Here's a fun case. A furniture company paid out higher commissions—are you starting to see the pattern?—to their salespeople for selling a new high-tech line of office furniture.

Sales reps who sold 210 units on one contract made more per unit than those who sold 21. Sounds fair, doesn't it? But when asked how much more work it took to sell the larger amount, reps said, "Honestly, it's the same."

On further investigation, another group of people was discovered who had considerable influence on whether the reps made the sale: the designers. The designers were not highly motivated to create a schematic, a diagram of how the prospect could use the furniture. It required a lot of effort. Yet this had to happen before the sale could be made.

When the designers saw how critical their role was to making sales, their motivation for creating schematics improved greatly. The company reinforced this new focus by rewarding the designers for their teamwork in closing sales. You can guess what happened next: Sales are now on their way up. Mystery solved.

Maximize Your Mix

I hope I've disqualified cash in your mind as an effective reward. And I hope you've learned what until now has been a well-kept secret: The high-performance mix simply does not substitute compensation for rewards.

Your mix won't be exactly the same as that of another company. Since you're probably already compensating your people at about the right level for your market, you just need to add the right mix of rewards and recognition.

Put on your trench coat and don't be afraid to investigate. Search out the specific behaviors it takes to get the results you need. Reward people who show improvement in those behaviors and recognize those who produce results.

It'd be a crying shame to waste your money on the wrong mix.

Notes

[1]"More Proof that Non-cash Awards are More Motivating than Cash," *Incentive,* May 1997, 36.

[2]Vincent Alonzo, "Dollars and Sense," http://www.ossonline.com/dollars_and_sense3.html.

[3]"Don't Show Me the Money: New Study Reveals Cash Rewards Have No Lasting Value with Employees," http://64.70.236.152/articles/a12.htm.

[4]"Cash vs. Merchandise," *Partners for Incentives,* January 2003, 2.

[5]*Managers* were also rewarded for observing reps' behaviors. Specifically, how were reps doing at building relationships during the first 30 seconds of the call? *Teams* were rewarded for the number of products sold per order (solution selling).

6

GET THE MOST FOR YOUR MONEY

Since most managers responsible for reward strategies have to cover their bottom—line, that is, I thought I'd focus one chapter on getting the greatest results for your money.

The secret, as you can tell by the illustration, is to look for funding in unlikely places. Then, while others are still watching where they step, you can bag up the byproducts of your program (revenue increases, cost savings) and turn them into even more gold. Here's some fertilizer for thought, in the form of Frequently Asked Questions.

Q: My boss says she's already paying people good money to do their jobs. Why should she reward them for something they should be doing anyway?

A: In a perfect world, every employee would be a wild-eyed overachiever. Since we don't live in a perfect world, the Eighty Percent Club mostly just shows up and gets the job done. Rewards help shift more people into the group of superheroes who are already getting top results.

I hope you've gotten the point that a reward program—or any performance improvement program, for that matter—is not a strategic goal.

Rewards help you *accelerate* results toward your strategic goals by keeping more people focused on the behaviors that achieve those results. Most people's performance will improve significantly and quickly when they know exactly what to do, and many more will join the ranks of your top performers.

A fraction of these combined gains will cover the costs of the rewards paid out for improvement. Generally, you can expect 200 percent to 1,000 percent ROI because, even when the reward is taken away, people continue to perform the Call to Action behaviors. People don't get tired of doing what works.

Q: I'm tired of rewarding the same people over and over. Call me a cheapskate, but I don't want to reward my top performers for results they would've produced anyway.

A: Sorry if I'm being redundant, but here's the key: Reward *everyone* for improvement, and recognize top performers for results.

Now I'm not suggesting that your top performers shouldn't get the maximum reward. They work hard for it. They deserve it. In fact, top performers, typically your top 10 percent, should receive their reward for improvement like everyone else, *plus* special recognition. That recognition can take the form of travel and other exclusive benefits.

What I *am* suggesting is that you get all of your players involved in achieving the Call to Action and help them make incremental gains, rewarding them along the way instead of at the end of the game.

Q: I'm not a psychic. How am I supposed to know which behaviors will get the greatest results?

A: Figure out what your top performers are doing to get results—their best practices—then clone those behaviors.

Look at your data to find out who is improving. Who's earning *e*Points for achieving the behaviors in your Call to Action? Who is getting results early in the program?

Now, ask your top performers the intelligent questions we discussed in Chapter 4:
- How's it going?
- What is contributing to your success?

- What are your obstacles?
- Hmmm. Any other obstacles?
- If you had a magic wand and could add, change or delete anything today, what would it be?

Once you've figured out the specific things they are doing that others aren't, clone those behaviors. By cloning, I mean communicating them to the rest of the team so they can copy them and accelerate achieving the Call to Action.

Oh, and one more thing: Don't forget to recognize those who share the secrets of their success.

Q: I can't afford to reward everybody. So where should I focus rewards first?

A: Remember your magic-wand wish? Find out who's helping you get your wish and make them happy that they are doing it.

Organizations often overlook three categories of people whose behaviors can have a tremendous impact on sales and customer relationships: managers, administrative support people and service associates such as drivers and installers.

Typically, you'll want to look at the group of people with the greatest impact on revenue. In the "Long story short" below, the largest group had the greatest impact, but you'll usually find that you can start your program with a select group that's having significant impact.

Long story short: Sometimes the answer will surprise you.
A bank had been rewarding platform bankers for increasing sales. Most of the bank's branches were seriously under goal. But there were two branches that consistently turned in results far over their goals. The regional president focusing on sales was frustrated. He knew that if two branches could do it, hundreds of others should be able to as well.

The regional president asked me to help him determine what these high-performing platform bankers were doing that worked so well. On further investigation, we discovered that every Monday afternoon the platform bankers held a meeting and offered their teller groups an incentive based on this Call to Action:

Call to Action – Sales

- **Magic-wand wish:** Close the performance gap (as measured by cross-sales) between high-performing and low-performing branches.
- **Behavior:** Ask the customer a standard, open-ended question regarding seasonal interests such as the purchase of a new car, the graduation of a child, plans for a home renovation project and so forth, as verified by supervisor observation.
- **Behavior:** Establish rapport with the customer by relating your own personal story regarding a wedding or graduation in your family or your own child starting school, as verified by supervisor observation.
- **Result:** Refer the customer to a platform banker to close the sale on a specific service or product.

The regional president replicated this Call to Action among all the branches. The Call to Action depended on a *team* (the tellers *and* the platform bankers) to cross-sell additional products and services to customers. Previously, the bank had rewarded only the platform bankers for making sales. Now they began to reward the *tellers* for their critical role in making the sales.

Soon the entire organization began to enjoy sustained growth. The pre-program average was 15 closed sales per team member. The post-program average was 26 closed sales per team member— a 58% improvement!

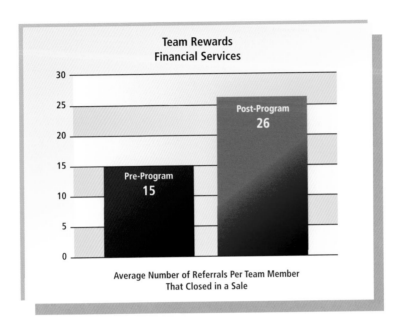

Team Rewards
Financial Services

Post-Program
26

Pre-Program
15

Average Number of Referrals Per Team Member
That Closed in a Sale

Q: Should managers get rewards too, or do they have to be good for nothing?

A: If you need managers to behave differently so employees will behave differently, put a reward on managers' heads, too.

Let's say a sales manager is required to ride along with each of her reps on three customer appointments in the first 30 days of a reward program. The manager's job is to evaluate the rep's performance, give him or her feedback and reinforce improvement that meets Call to Action criteria, by rewarding *e*Points on the spot.

As the manager rides along with 10 different reps, she will be learning from the top performers and coaching everyone to the highest standards she observes. This is management behavior that should be rewarded.

Many companies, however, reward managers on the performance of their reps without regard to the managers' own performance. A manager may get 125 percent of her team's earnings without necessarily having done anything herself to earn the reward. In fact, the manager may be working the top performers for all they're worth, while others with enormous potential sit on the bench.

What happens when the manager is rewarded for her team's revenue, whether the revenue came from the top three players or all 50? The manager gets the glory today, but the future of the team is in jeopardy, with three exhausted players and 47 who've never been challenged to deliver.

Long story short: Reward best practices in management. I worked with a large organization that had two branches on the East Coast that out-performed all the others. The two top-selling sales managers complained separately about the product managers who came into their offices and waved incentives in front of their salespeople to motivate them to sell their products.

After studying the situation, we realized that even though the company had just spent more than $2 million on consultative training for the salespeople, they were still allowing product managers to reward reps for selling their independent products rather than for making consultative sales, which produced higher revenue for the company.

The two high-performing sales managers were doing something the other managers were not doing—and they both happened to be doing the same thing, even though they had not compared notes: They were keeping the product managers out and reinforcing their reps for consultative selling behaviors that yielded the desired results.

These two top sales managers, even without the "help" of the product managers, had far and away the highest sales of the products being promoted. Even more important, they had the highest revenue per call and highest, most consistent sales growth.

The moral of the story: Don't forget to reward managers when you discover that their behaviors are helping them motivate and retain top talent and get stellar results.

Q: **Where can I get the fastest wins with a reward program?**

A: **Start where you're already making the most money. Figure out the behaviors that got those results and get more people to behave the same way.**

If you've ever taken a golf lesson, you know that if you try to concentrate on your stance, your grip and your backswing all at once, you will look like a contortionist—and likely whiff the ball. Whoops.

Many companies strike a similar pose when they consider how to accomplish their strategic goals. Take accounts receivable, for instance. Most AR departments staff at more than 100 percent to fill the seats of reps who are out or on vacation. They typically depend on collecting money quickly by making brief, unfriendly calls every so often (usually at dinner time) after bills are sent.

AR associates, like novice golfers, are often asked to improve on several metrics at once: collecting current debt; 30-days-plus, 60-days-plus and 90-days-plus debt; and bad debt. They also may be asked to increase calls per day and/or reduce talk time on each call. That's seven metrics!

Have you ever been called and barked at about how much you owe on a bill? Sorry, I know you pay your bills on time. But you can imagine what that would be like.

Wouldn't it make more sense to observe what top-collecting reps do and help the others copy those behaviors and activities?

One AR department did just that and found that the top-performing rep had unique ways of establishing rapport with customers during the first 30 seconds of each call. The department was able to copy the rep's style, with incredible results.

The time value of the money gained by earlier collections and reduced bad debt covered the cost of the program. The success required fewer calls, which meant less overtime and resulted in great savings.

Q: When I was daydreaming in a meeting, I got elected to sell the idea of rewards to management. How can I show that the potential gains outweigh the risks?

A: Add up the dollars you can realistically expect to earn from a reward program. Then subtract the projected cost of the program. The difference is the program's potential ROI, which should knock the bosses' socks off.

If this sounds like lemonade-stand math, it is, but on a larger scale and with more powerful results.

The table below shows a hypothetical budget based on a sales scenario. These amounts are based on actual results from hundreds of sales programs, although each program varies greatly.

If you believe you cannot justify the expense of a program, don't forget your greatest risk: the cost of doing nothing. If you do nothing, not only do you forfeit the incremental margin gain or cost savings, you lose the performance improvement that lasts long after an effective reward program goes away.

Step 1. Estimate your maximum budget. As a guideline, your total budget should be about 10% of your participants' base compensation. Therefore, in a sales force of 250 whose average annual pay is $50,000, you can expect that expenses will not exceed $1,250,000 (250 x $5,000).	$1,250,000 Projected Budget
Step 2. Project incremental margin. Project sales lift or cost savings at 5% to 10% improvement over trend (we'll use 10% here for ease of calculation, and assume a recent trend of 0%). If the average lift of 10% equals $20,000 monthly in margin, the incremental margin gain is $240,000 annually ($20,000 x 12 months). $240,000 x 250 people = $60,000,000 x 10% improvement = $6,000,000	$6,000,000 Projected Incremental Margin
Step 3. Calculate investment required.	
A. Fixed costs. Fixed costs (communications, administration and tracking systems) should require 10% to 15% of the projected budget. We'll use the worst-scenario cost of 15% (.15 x $1,250,000 = $187,500).	$187,500
B. Projected reward budget. Estimate rewards at 10% of average compensation, paid to 60% to 80% of your participants. In a sales force of 250, you can expect to reward 125-212 (we'll figure on the average168) employees at some level. If their rewards average 10% of average base compensation (.10 x $50,000 = $5,000), including tax liability, your reward budget will be $840,000 ($5,000 x 168 employees).	$840,000
Investment (Cost of program)	$1,027,500
Step 4. Calculate ROI.	
A. Subtract cost of program from projected incremental margin to get ROI in dollars. $6,000,000 - $1,027,500 = $4,972,500	$4,972,500
B. Divide dollar ROI by cost of program to calculate projected ROI $4,972,500 / $1,027,500. Now that's investing your money wisely!	484%

Typically, you can project incremental margin gain or cost savings from a reward program at 5 percent to 10 percent over current trend (see table). **This is also your cost of doing nothing.**

Guideline – Your range of current performance is your range of opportunity. Remember, I am talking about how to accelerate the achievement of this year's business strategies. A reward program is not always the answer.

For sales, if the difference between high performers and middle performers is 100% or more, the program will probably pay for itself. In other words, if high performers (the top 10%) are at 125% of quota and middle performers (the Eighty Percent Club) are at 75% of quota, a 50-point difference, you may want to reconsider.

I base this projection on my experience that about 60% to 80% of the middle performers will improve enough to earn rewards (about 5% over their current performance), funding the program through incremental gains.

In service companies, the difference between high and middle performers can be as little as 10% and still fund the program. This is because when margins are greater and lost sales more costly, it doesn't take nearly as many wins to earn back your investment in a program.

Q: What are some places that most people don't think about looking for funding?

A: As the first manure entrepreneur discovered, there's hidden value even in things that seem to have no connection with money. If you're determined enough, you can sniff them out.

First, consider the projected incremental gains from:
- Increased sales and/or reduced costs (see table at left)
- Reduced turnover and associated training and ramp-up
- Decreased overtime
- Reduced call loads (because of first-call resolution)
- Lower staffing to handle call loads

Because you will be rewarding the early behaviors that lead to bottom-line results, and constantly improving on those behaviors, you can count on greater incremental gains than you would achieve with a traditional program.

Second, most organizations have funds in areas such as marketing, training and "miscellaneous" categories that potentially can be earmarked for reward programs. With a little creativity, executives can partner across functional lines in the interests of increasing revenue.

A third source of funding that is often used for rewards is profit sharing. It often becomes a form of "compensation," since employees learn to expect their share of the bonus. But it's fair to offer a percentage of it in the form of rewards that, after all, everyone has the opportunity to earn.

Cash in on Fast Results

Once you get your "cash cow" working for you, the byproduct of your program—more revenue—provides fertile ground (if you catch my drift) for the next round of rewards. You can keep raising the bar on the same behaviors and activities until you reach a plateau. Take a break for a couple of months, and then develop a new Call to Action. I haven't found a corporate leader yet who didn't want (and need!) to improve.

Now that you know how to turn expenses into assets, we're ready to talk about the rewards themselves. Bet you thought I'd forgotten about those.

7

{ *Principle 6* }

MAKE SURE YOUR REWARDS
ARE REWARDING

You might think a book on rewards would talk a lot about rewards. But remember, I'm not talking about traditional reward programs. I'm talking about using rewards to accelerate profits NOW. And I believe the main thing about rewards is that they should be rewarding.

But trying to guess what a particular person will find rewarding is like trying to forecast the weather. And we all know how accurate weather forecasters are.

I do have some thoughts (no surprise to you) on how to make rewards more rewarding, and this chapter covers three main ways:
   1. Give people a choice.
   2. Catch people doing things right (random reinforcement).
   3. Combine individual and team rewards.

1. Give People a Choice

So many programs fizzle when the managers choose a reward that floats *their* boat—only to find that the salespeople would prefer just about anything to an Alaskan cruise that keeps them away from home another week; and the support people aren't exactly ecstatic about fly-fishing equipment.

The key to rewards, as I said, is to make them rewarding. And the only way to do that is to give people a choice.

When they can choose among a Caribbean cruise, a big-screen television, a bedroom set and diamond earrings, it gives them a chance to set their own goals. Rewards become a means to an end. As people see their goal coming within reach, they can't wait to ask, "What do I need to do next?"

Let's Trash Cash, One More Time

 You're watching "Wheel of Fortune" on television. The brilliant contestant asks for an "S." The buzzer sounds. That letter has already been chosen and the play moves to someone else. When the play comes back around, though, the same contestant asks for an "S" again. What is wrong with this picture? The stress of being on national television must've wiped out this person's hard drive.

Yet organizations do this every day. Even though they already have commission (cash) at risk, when managers want salespeople to sell more, what do they do? They put more commission at risk! In this case, "S" does not stand for smart.

Did I mention that cash is not a good accelerator? If you put a higher commission on a product, sure, people will sell that product. But will they keep selling the bread-and-butter stuff you need them to sell every day?

I've found that people do what makes sense to them. And it makes more sense to sell the products that net them a higher commission. Why should they bust their buns doing something that doesn't bring them the maximum reward?

Rewards Я Us

Speaking of rewards, here's a brief review of the standard reward options:

Sweepstakes. Managers often think they can choose the best reward, and sweepstakes are tempting because the reward cost is supposedly contained. But not everyone *wants* the Mustang convertible or the trip to Las Vegas. Even worse, what if your lowest performer wins it? Sometimes a sweeps can end up *costing* instead of saving you money, not to mention causing you to lose face. Yikes!

Gift certificates. If you can get people to set a goal for what they'll do with their gift certificate, this can be a good option. Otherwise, it lacks trophy value—a gift card isn't something most people display in their homes. And it takes effort to redeem the certificate. You wouldn't give one to the Queen of England, would you? Ho-hum.

You may be asking: Doesn't cash give people the ultimate choice?
Well, I have to admit that, technically, it does. **But** research shows that cash does not have the motivational power of tangible rewards. Not only that, if you take cash away, it feels like a cut in pay. Remember entitlement?

In a well-known article titled "The Trouble with Money," which appeared in *Incentive* magazine,[1] Goodyear Tire and Rubber Company ran a controlled study comparing the results of cash and non-cash rewards.

With guidance from its marketing research department, the company stack-ranked its 60 retail districts and divided them into two groups by odd and even numbers to ensure impartiality. One group was arbitrarily chosen to receive cash, the other, reward points redeemable for merchandise.

While the sales results of both groups improved, the non-cash group surpassed the cash group by nearly 50%. The data was determined 95% statistically significant.

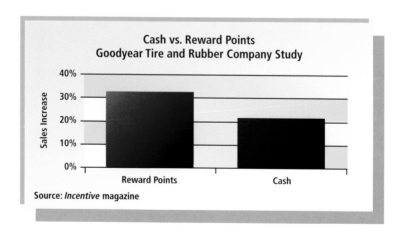

Source: *Incentive* magazine

Cash/debit cards. In my view, a real reward is one that you don't have to work to redeem. You don't have to take your cash or your debit card and go shopping. Cash and debit cards often get spent on cleaning supplies, gas or food. A reward should be more fun than that.

Not only is there no trophy value, cash rewards are often perceived as (you can probably complete the sentence by now) *an entitlement.* You may be able to pull off an exciting launch with cash-type rewards, but after a few weeks there's only one word for them. Boring.

Group and individual travel. This can be an inspiring reward—one that involves the family in setting a goal and motivates the employee to go for it.

Be aware. Group travel may be a treat for the spouses or friends of salespeople. It's a once-in-a-lifetime experience designed to honor the employee, in the company of significant others and executives. But another trip may be the last thing the salesperson wants to take. You may want to give them an option to redeem travel points for merchandise. Slam-dunk.

Lifestyle rewards. You know how I feel about cash. But some companies are successfully using cash for lifestyle rewards. When your top performers hit a certain level, you can offer them a points multiplier, say 1.25, and let them choose an approved personal reward that doesn't involve installment payments. It could be cosmetic surgery, the contracting for an addition on their home, or college tuition. Yippee!

Merchandise selection. Now, as you know, this is the most appropriate all-around reward. It's flexible. It's fun. It's dream-worthy. Your new jet ski is delivered to your home and assembled. You've been thinking about it for months, and it's yours, all yours. You picked it out. Your friends and loved ones have been watching you get closer and closer. Now they have the pleasure of sharing in your excitement. Wahoo!

2. Catch People Doing Things Right

This is where I talk about random reinforcement, the best motivator of all. Random reinforcement is simply another way of saying, "Inspect what you expect." If you catch employees doing something right and reward them on the spot, publicly, they catch on to the goals with lightning speed. And so does everyone who's watching them.

Of course, there's the danger that your managers won't be consistent in catching and rewarding people, and their actions will be perceived as favoritism.

Remember when your teacher told you exactly what you'd have to do to earn an "A"? The unions will be especially interested to know that criteria are well defined and that everyone will have three (or six or whatever number you choose) opportunities to earn *e*Points. They'll want to know that everyone who is randomly checked receives feedback each time, whether or not they meet the criteria for getting the reinforcement.

A national copying chain gave reps eight opportunities to be reinforced by managers who rode along with them on sales appointments. Smart reps set up *more* than eight ride-alongs to give themselves more chances to earn the reinforcement.

The criterion was an excellent (as opposed to good) customer profile, a document that reps completed after an appointment. Clear examples of excellent profiles were given. Managers could tell by the profile how well the reps had done their homework on the customer.

Here are some other examples of random reinforcement: supervisors listening to customer service reps as they take phone calls or a supervisor observing how a teller handles customers. In both cases, if the employee meets the criteria for success, the manager hands the employee a certificate for reward points and publicly commends him or her for a fine job.

Innovative companies allow employees to recognize each other in the same way, and some even change the recognized behaviors from week to week. Everyone learns to watch for the valued behaviors. Peer recognition creates a culture of celebration.

Clone Good Managers—What a Novel Idea

How do you get non-participative managers on board for random reinforcement? Let's go back to the cloning concept. An upper-level manager finds a few top-performing managers who use random reinforcement well. Then the upper-level manager figures out how to publicize those successes.

The exec may hold a conference call to talk about the success of those groups, or make data available showing how those managers are achieving better results. The top-performing managers share specific things they are doing to get the lift. When other managers raise objections (We just don't have time for that!), the top performers can talk about how they overcame those same obstacles.

The key is to have some kind of indicator showing which managers are using the tools and which aren't so that managers on the next level up can coach those who aren't on board.

Which brings me back to a point I made earlier: If success depends in part on the managers, be sure to sweeten the pot for them, too. Reward them for doing the ride-alongs. Or reward them based on a pre-determined percentage of employees who demonstrate their knowledge by passing the required quizzes or who successfully sell a mix of products and services.

Catch the managers doing something right. Now there's a thought for the future.

3. Combine Individual and Team Rewards

Why reward teams? One good reason is to cross-pollinate ideas. Team rewards get groups teaching each other and sharing with one another. People learn at different rates, and team members who are getting results faster can show others how they're doing it.

A few quick tips for team rewards:

As a general rule, reward *individuals* for behaviors and *teams* for results.

Maybe I'm starting to sound like a scratched CD, but I can't emphasize enough how important it is to think in terms of your *Call to Action* (two behaviors and one result). It's no different for teams. A few examples:

• **Call center.** You may reward *individuals* for engaging the customer in the first 30 seconds of the call and knowing where to find answers to customers' questions. The *team* (in this case, the entire center) is rewarded for increases in first-pass resolution or customer satisfaction scores.

- **Warehouse.** You might reward *individuals* who wear back supports and work out at the gym to strengthen their backs, and reward the *team* for lower Workmen's Compensation costs.

- **Small teams.** On teams that combine sales and technical roles, you may want to reward *individuals* for demonstrating team-related skills such as collaboration and knowledge sharing, and reward the *team* as a whole for increased sales.

Reward teams when different job functions are needed to achieve the results.

For instance, there's a salesperson in the field, an engineering consultant who helps propose and close the sale, then others who deliver and/or install the equipment. If any of these people does a poor job, you'll have unhappy customers and higher overhead. Therefore, it's smart to motivate the entire team to engage and deploy quickly. That's how you accelerate profits NOW.

Pay attention to fairness.

Everyone seems to have an eagle eye for fairness. Here are three ways to make teams fair:

1. Follow the leader. Remember the playground? Everyone wants the skilled players. Make sure the average results of the performers on each team are equal to your location average. And try to get a top performer on each team. That way the best team's average performance can become the average of the organization.

2. Clone best practices. An engineer assigned to support several salespeople may favor one over the others. This is a good time to ask those intelligent questions you learned back in Chapter 4 to find out what makes the engineer and that particular salesperson a good team.

You'll probably find that the salesperson is good at planning, knows her customers' needs, and happens to close more sales this particular engineer works on. Who wouldn't want to work with her?

Now's your opportunity to clone those best practices. Reward salespeople who create good customer profiles and who get the engineer involved. Reward the entire team—sales, support and logistics people—for the closed sales resulting from their pre-sale collaboration.

3. Expand the team. If a location or distributor resists being divided into teams, consider the entire location a team.

Switch it up.

In fact, since you're taking my advice in the future and running shorter programs, you can base some programs on rewarding individuals, others on rewarding small teams, location teams or a combination. The main thing is to get everyone engaged in everyone else's improvement.

Celebrate.

The biggest reason to reward teams is that you get to celebrate together. In addition to group celebration, be sure to let team members recognize and reward each other during the program. After all, who wants to party by themselves? A great second reason to celebrate is that it's a cheap and effective way to communicate the goals and the success of the program—again.

> **Long story short: Reward teams for saving money.** A major agricultural distributor started rewarding its warehouse crew as a team when the company realized how much workers depended on each other to get the job done and keep costs down.
>
> The picker was doing a good job of loading heavy goods on bottom and lighter ones on top. The truck loader, however, was packing the items so close together that bags of grain rubbed against one another, spilling their contents.
>
> The spills attracted mice. The mice did what they do after they eat. Customers refused to pay for entire loads.
>
> Only the head of damaged goods had the numbers, so it took a little investigating to figure out the problem. Once managers figured out the roles of the warehouse people, the company began to reward individuals for paying attention to details, and the team as a whole for bringing down costs on damaged and returned items. Costs dropped dramatically.

Rewards: The Result Accelerators

Well, that's everything you always wanted to know about rewards, but were afraid to ask. (But aren't you glad I told you anyway?) In the next chapter, we'll check the dashboard gauges to see how your program's going. Then we'll let you get back to the future and plan your next program to accelerate results.

Notes

[1] Tom K. Gravalos and John M. Jack, "The Trouble with Money," www.biperformance.com\servebi\money.pdf.

8

{ *Principle 7* }

CHECK YOUR FOCUS

You've learned how to avoid the two most common mistakes managers make with rewards: leaving a program in place for a long time (more than six months) and using compensation as a reward.

You've also thought about how to fund rewards and where to find the money.

Now, before you launch your program, you'll need a checklist so you don't make any of the common pre-trip and in-flight mistakes that cause programs to crash and burn. This checklist encompasses some key topics that, considered carefully, will help you maintain a sharper focus.

 1. One more time: Does this reward initiative support our corporate strategy?

Surprisingly, this is not as much of a gimme as you might think. Often, the noble intention to focus on strategy gets lost in the shuffle of putting together the rewards, the budget, the administration and tracking, and the communications.

So, before takeoff, it's important to ask again, "Does this support my strategy?"

Some managers get carried away and begin putting separate rewards on each strategy. Remember, rewards are simply accelerators to focus attention on the *behaviors* that will help you accomplish your strategies.

Your reward program should help you pilot your organization to its destination via the most direct route, with rewards along the way to speed up the flight. Think of rewards as a high-performance jet fuel that helps you get to the right place at the right time.

If this is as far as you get on the checklist, it could be worth a bundle in cost savings and reduced headaches. But a good pilot doesn't take shortcuts when it comes to the public's safety, so don't skip the next items on the list.

Long story short: All for one. Believe it or not, you may be able to address all or most of your strategic initiatives with one reward program.

For example, one financial services executive had six strategies, as far-flung as deploying a CRM system and training all employees on it, de-layering management, adding a new portfolio management product and, of course, increasing sales.

He was planning to build separate reward programs for each strategy until he realized that most of them shared one common denominator: The goal was to improve customer service. Let's look at his Call to Action:

Call to Action - Bridging
- **Magic-wand wish:** Move from a service to a sales-and-service culture.
- **Behavior:** Demonstrate knowledge of 1) CRM and 2) portfolio management product, as verified by completion of quizzes.
- **Behavior:** Demonstrate ability to complete accurate profile on 10 targeted customers using new tool for identifying products and services that would benefit the customer, as verified by manager's evaluation.
- **Result:** Close three sales of the new portfolio management product within first 90 days.

Not only did this executive save oodles of money by running one reward initiative instead of six, the employees clearly saw how the tools could assist them in helping their customers.

2. Will managers coach and reinforce the behaviors we've defined?

Now I'm not saying that 100 percent of your managers will get on board for a program. But I recommend that you focus on manager buy-in with a passion until you have at least a third who are believers. As the others observe the higher results those managers are getting, they'll get on board too.

One program rewarded salespeople for their knowledge of a new "solution selling" process. To receive a reward, the rep's manager had to ride along and evaluate how the rep handled the call. Reps could be rewarded up to eight times per month for excellent—not average or good—calls. Excellent calls were clearly defined.

As you can imagine, this meant managers had to do a lot of ride-alongs. Some of the managers took the easy route and rated reps as excellent without actually going on the calls with the reps. Were the reps unhappy? You bet. They reported the managers, who were fired.

If managers are required to change their behaviors, make sure there's something in it for them, too. Educate them and help them see the benefits of changing their behavior and helping others to change theirs. Show them how this initiative will make their lives easier in the long term.

Also, don't believe what managers say. Some will claim they are supportive of the new effort. **But watch what they do.** If rewards are not getting paid out, or if your numbers are going down instead of up, you're losing altitude and you'd better take corrective action fast.

Finally, make sure managers are rewarding for *improvement,* not for goal attainment. There may be some resistance at first to rewarding less-than-stellar performance. That's why baselines for performance and criteria for rewards need to be crystal clear. Are you also beginning to see the need for clear and repeated communications about the program and for feedback on how people are doing?

3. Will managers enforce the consequences?

This is one flight that has set departure and arrival times, and a charted course. We're not dilly-dallying, doing air tricks and forgetting to look for the landing strip. There's no time to lose. But deadlines and targeted landings are meaningless if they get moved. And the temptation for managers is to move them.

One reason managers make allowances is that they don't believe in the Call to Action criteria (see Checklist Item 5). Make sure you can look at yourself in the mirror after you've set the criteria because you're the one who'll have to enforce them.

I've found the acid test is to run the details past a few top performers and their managers to find the loopholes. This is great contingency planning.

Assuming your Call to Action criteria are fair, verifiable and well communicated, don't bend the rules.

"But …." Everyone has an excuse: "The computer for the demo was in Chicago"; "The data was dirty"; "My partner was ill."

Excuse me if I sound heartless, but the deadline was either met or it was not. The behavior was demonstrated or it was not. The results were achieved or they were not. People are being paid and rewarded to solve problems, think ahead and make back-up plans.

Does this remind you of your kids—or your own shenanigans (in the distant past of course)? If you extend a deadline once, people will look for workarounds on every future initiative. Have courage and stand firm. Don't bend the rules.

 ## 4. Have we created an environment among the managers that supports the change?

Since a behavior-change program is different from the traditional reward programs managers have come to know and love, it will take some effort to make the cultural shift required—and as always, it starts with management.

Managers often have weekly or monthly meetings to talk about results. They may look at the stack rankings of the sales offices or customer service teams and ask, "What's new?" They're looking at marketing efforts, customer satisfaction index scores, budget-to-expense ratios and revenue growth—reports that are already in print.

The missing link is behaviors—living, changing behaviors. Behaviors that will accelerate profits this week.

Rarely do managers take the extra few minutes required to discuss the best practices, those behaviors that are getting higher performance—which usually translates to *higher lift*—at some locations. It may seem like a subtle difference, but it's an important one.

Here's a simple way to get at the behaviors that are getting the highest lift in your top locations:

- Ask your high-performing location: "What are the best practices that got you the highest lift in this location?"
- Ask other locations: "Do you think you can copy those? If not, how can we help you remove the obstacles to doing that?"

The goal is to transfer new knowledge gained so that everyone can use the best practices *now* to achieve your strategies. In other words, the lift is in cloning the behaviors that are getting you the improvement. This often begins with manager-to-manager coaching.

Before you take off on a new route, be sure you file a new flight plan.

Long story short: Union rewards. One manager who had made the transition to behaviors learned to look for the sales office that had the greatest lift. He asked the manager of that office what they were doing. Here's the conference call they had:

Manager: What are you doing to get such good results?

High performer: We're noticing that the people who've passed their knowledge quizzes have the highest performance, so we're looking at what they're doing.

Low performer: Well, I could talk about quizzes all day long, but my people don't have time to take quizzes.

High performer: We don't either.

Low performer: Well, when are people taking the quizzes then?

High performer: On their lunch break, at home, during down times.

Low performer: We can't do that. We have a union shop.

High performer: So? We have a union shop too. We're giving them every resource they can put their hands on, and top performers know that if they put in extra time and effort, they can take their results to new levels. Isn't that why the company put the rewards in place—to point people in the right direction so they can get the knowledge they need to be better at their jobs?

Manager to low performer: Do you think you could do this?

Low performer: How can we do it without having a union grievance filed?

On the phone, the top-performing manager coached the low-performing one on how to ask for the new behaviors without provoking a union grievance. By the following week, the low-performing office's knowledge, as demonstrated by their quiz completion rate, had taken off. **The company's sales growth exceeded 20%.**

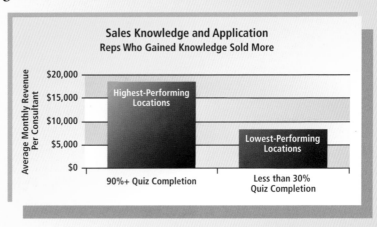

Sales Knowledge and Application
Reps Who Gained Knowledge Sold More

5. Are the criteria for the Call to Action verifiable?

If you, the manager, can't verify the criteria you've set up for your Call to Action, you're in trouble even before your program gets off the ground. No one would get on a plane if they knew it had mechanical problems. Don't expect your employees to do so, either.

I've defined the Call to Action, for the sake of simplicity, as two behaviors and one result. It's impossible to reward those who achieve the Call to Action unless each of these elements is verifiable.

Verifying Behaviors

Let's look at some examples of behaviors that are verifiable through observation:

- **Engaging with the customer in first 30 seconds of a call.** The manager observes against a well-defined set of phrases and/or communication techniques.

- **Listening to a customer and bridging to the product need or the conclusion of the call.** The manager observes against a set of specific questions that must be asked, and verifies confirmations back to the customer.

- **Completing specified criteria for an excellent presentation.** The manager uses a checklist to verify that all criteria are met.

Other behaviors are verifiable through more objective means.

- **Knowledge.** You can verify a salesperson's level of motivation by the rate at which he or she takes required online quizzes. You can also verify whether people are engaged by the number of tries it takes them to pass their quizzes. By the way, I don't consider knowledge synonymous with training (see box on page 86).

- **Appointments with decision makers—Presidents, VPs and Cs (CEOs, CIOs and CFOs).** Verify the time and date.

Verifying Results

It's easier to measure results criteria. You can count them. A couple of examples:

- **Sales.** Sales of a targeted product or of bundled services and/or products.

- **Service.** Mean time to repair (technicians); first-pass resolution (customer service).

The key, as I've mentioned throughout this book, is to avoid putting the reward solely on completed sales or customer satisfaction score improvements. Those results take time to accomplish, and sometimes it's hard to tell exactly who did the critical work to accomplish the lift—or, if you didn't get any improvement, what needs to change. You end up rewarding windfalls or people who just happened to be in the right place at the right time.

Knowledge and training are different.
Throughout this book, I've talked about rewarding people for knowledge. Most companies realize the importance of training, and invest heavily in helping people learn job- and customer-related skills.

In contrast, knowledge helps people combine what they've learned about products and customers, and apply those learnings to come up with a solution for each customer's needs. The employee's mantra for attaining knowledge is this:

Knowledge Mantra
- When I speak with customers, what do I need to listen for?
- What do I need to know about my products and services?
- How do I combine what I've learned in those two areas into a solution that fits this specific customer?

I believe the successful companies in the coming years will be those that create an environment for their employees to learn fast, and then immediately use what they learn in order to meet customers' needs better than their competitors can. The creative use of online quizzes is an inexpensive way to transfer and validate knowledge. The intravenous drip...drip...drip of four questions a week is usually more effective than a four-hour mega-dose of training.

6. Is your tracking simple and meaningful to the individuals you're asking to change?

Often, the tracking mechanism is meaningful only to the managers who are asking people to change. For example, how much did we sell last week? What was our customer satisfaction score?

These numbers mean nothing to the individuals who are being asked to change. The numbers don't tell them anything about how to improve personally.

Here's a good exercise. Try performing the exact behaviors you'll be asking of your people. It may sound funny or feel funny the first time, but it will give you instant empathy for what your people will have to go through to achieve the Call to Action.

If you don't have a mechanism for tracking your critical behaviors, create one. It can be as simple as a checklist or as complicated as a relational database. But you have to measure or observe the behaviors and the results that comprise your Call to Action. Or expect your program never to leave the runway.

7. Is your program fair?

Since everyone wants a fair program, this checkpoint item is probably already top of mind. Just a few cautions:

Be aware of gaming laws. Some states have gaming laws that change from county to county. If you are using a sweepstakes, make sure your program is in compliance in every location before take-off.

Don't set up undue competition among peers. A lot of managers think competition is a good thing, but it causes hard feelings and inhibits the sharing of best practices. Why would managers or top performers give away their secrets of success when others can take the big prize away from them? And without best practices, how can you repeat stellar results? Get your team performing against the real rivals—your competitors.

Think twice before running a sweepstakes contest. Many companies try to reduce reward costs by running a sweepstakes. Or they think winning a big prize is more motivating (even though not everyone loves the prize being offered—see Chapter 7). The biggest pitfall with a sweepstakes drawing is that you may draw the name of your lowest performer. That person wins the whole pot, which doesn't send a very positive message to those who worked hard but didn't win anything.

If you design a program based on behaviors that get results, it will pay for itself—*and* get the results. There is a limited risk that your program's results won't cover the projected cost of the rewards, but it's a far lesser risk than purchasing a big prize that not everyone wants or is able to earn.

Remember, in a union environment, rewards can be a great asset.
Unions usually require that a reward be made available to everyone. This is a positive, not a negative. You get the best results when you ask *everyone* to improve. If you could reward every employee who improved every day, think what a winning culture you would create.

8. Are you paying attention to your gauges?

When pilots run into bad weather, they watch their gauges and make course corrections that will get them to their destination.

During your program, you'll want to check certain indicators more often than others and make adjustments accordingly: How many are participating? Who is validating their knowledge by taking online quizzes and, more importantly, who's passing them? Are reward points being redeemed? Who are your early adapters and how can you use their best practices to get further improvements?

Oh, and by the way, what results are you getting? Of course, this is the most-watched indicator. If you're getting amazing results, you will be tempted to run the program longer. But please listen to the voice of experience: That is a bad idea. People will lose the sense of urgency and settle into old habits.

You'll find more about all of these gauges and the stories they tell in Chapter 9.

9. Do you have your celebration planned?

Passengers often applaud the pilot for a nice landing. In the case of a reward program, you'll want to do more than applaud. So give some thought to the celebration *before* take-off to make sure it will happen.

At program's end, share results and give people a chance to party. Recognize everyone who was involved and acknowledge the contribution they made to overall strategies. Remember, you're celebrating *improvement*. Even if the team fell short of the goal, you can recognize what they achieved.

This is the time to get re-energized and motivated to take on the next challenge. Don't blow it by throwing a wimpy party.

Flying Higher

Assuming you've passed all these checkpoints, it's time to put down your landing gear and get ready for a smooth landing and all-out celebration. Then you can take a brief break and get ready for the next flight, which should take you even higher—and to better places.

9

{ Principle 8 }

WATCH YOUR GAUGES
AND MAKE ADJUSTMENTS

When you think of a high-powered, sexy car, what comes to mind? James Bond's fantasy coupe? The Batmobile?

Allow me to suggest something more worthy of a NASCAR event (without the Viagra ads, of course). You want the lightest weight chassis and the simplest of dashboards—you can only focus on the essential metrics when you're moving at top speed.

When you're on the track, you're at the controls and you're going the right direction. To win the race, you need to know when to take the turns high, when to take them low. You want to take pit stops at strategic times.

In order to do these things, someone has to be watching the metrics and be aware of the mile markers. So you have your pit crew—usually your product marketing people—on the headphone telling you what's coming up and how to fine-tune your driving.

Let someone else do the analysis; you don't have time. But you'll want to watch the indicators for *yourself* to make sure you're achieving your company's strategy (notice I didn't say your personal goals). You'll watch the indicators for your *players* to keep them up to speed.

It won't take long for you to find yourself at the finish line at the head of the pack, with energy to spare for the next race.

What to Watch

Every indicator tells its own story, if you take time to pay attention. Here are a few key ones to watch:

1. How many people are playing?

I don't mean to insult your intelligence, but you wouldn't believe how many leaders don't pay any attention to this basic number. They start watching the finish line from day one, and if people aren't crossing the finish line a few days into the race, they put a bigger reward at the end of the race.

They don't bother to see who's left the starting line or made the first flag.

Participation is one indicator you should watch every day during the first 30 days of your program. How many people have registered on the program's Web site? How many have taken online quizzes to validate their knowledge? The more relational the database that drives your system, the higher quality indicators you'll have. But it need not be complicated.

If your participation is still low by the end of week two of a 60-day program—for most programs, less than 60 percent would qualify as low— you may want to check to see whether your launch was effective. Did a launch take place at all locations? Were your communications clear enough?

Go back and re-read Chapter 3 and consider sending a follow-up e-mail or holding a team meeting. Call your team to action—again.

2. Who's in the race?

While you're racing around the track, you'll also want to figure out who, exactly, is helping you achieve your strategy.

A lot of middle managers never even get a reward program off the starting line because they want to reward people who are three times removed from the strategy or from customers. They're still trying to figure out how to set up the rules while revenue opportunities—in the form of customers—are zipping by at top speed.

How do you figure out who's really in the race? You go to the top performers and ask them the intelligent questions, which are repeated on page 93. Your top performers will tell you who helped them hit their results.

Within the first 30 days of your program, you'll know who's really contributing and many times it's not the answer you expected. Often, as we discussed in Chapter 6, it's managers, support personnel or service employees. When you find out who they are, be sure to start rewarding them for the critical role they play.

3. Who's doing it best and why?

This is closely related to "Who's in the race?" but the focus here is on finding the top performers among all your participants. Again, you may be surprised when you find out who they are.

You want to look at who is earning reward points for achieving the Call to Action behaviors. This should be evident after about the first 15 to 30 days of the program. Look for the story in the numbers. Maybe it's one region, one market, one job function that's excelling. Take a pit stop now! Find out what they're doing that's putting them out in front.

What do you do next? Clone 'em and get 'em back in the race! You don't want to showcase your top performers and set up competition with them, but you do want to emphasize their *behaviors*. Talk to them about specifically what they are doing that gets results. These may be subtle behaviors underneath their success. Remember the intelligent questions from Chapter 4:

- How's it going?
- What's contributing to your success?
- What are your obstacles?
- Hmmm. Any other obstacles?
- If you had a magic wand and could add, change or delete anything today, what would it be?

If you ask nicely, people will share their knowledge. Then you can coach others to copy what's working and earn their own rewards. Once the whole team begins sharing knowledge and watching out for competitors, you can move up in the race even if you got off to a slow start.

Want to get some fast action? Post the stack rankings for all the locations. Let all the managers see who's achieving results and who's doing squat. You'll hear engines revving all around.

Quick tip: Since most programs require learning new products or processes, "Who's doing it best and why?" often translates to who's taking and passing their knowledge validation quizzes. It's an easy metric to check. If people aren't engaged, that may be a clue that participants don't really know what they need to do. Take time to clarify the Call to Action behaviors. And check to make sure the quizzes make sense. **Tell participants *exactly* what they need to do.**

Do you see how reward programs, correctly designed, can create momentum for innovation? Participants try things they've never considered, ideas that take you to the next level. Now you're racing with the big dogs.

4. How fast are people hitting the mile markers?

Now that you know who's participating and who's doing it best and why, you'll want to be aware of who reaches the mile markers the fastest. You watch this metric by paying attention to who starts earning reward points first.

Throughout the program, you'll encourage everyone to use the techniques used by these early adapters to get the same results they're getting. As people receive feedback on their performance, the buzz about what works ratchets up performance from the individual to the team, the location, the district, the region, the organization. When you're ready to plan your next program, you'll recalibrate your baseline and raise the bar. **This is the formula for permanent behavior change.**

A common allegation is that once you take the reward away, people will quit performing. This may be true if you reward people only at the end of the race, as most traditional programs do. But if you reward for your Call to Action behaviors—your mile markers—people know exactly what to do to get results.

Salespeople, for example, have learned how to write an excellent profile and get the subject matter expert involved in the proposal process. If those things are earning them more sales (and more commissions), why would they revert back to their old ways? Remember the case study on page 20 in which a company's results held steady, even during the months no reward was offered?

5. What improvement did we get over the last lap?

Now that you're more tuned in to the key indicators, you're ready to focus on how well you've done in the race. Results are the most basic metric, the speedometer on your high-powered racecar. You've been watching them as mile markers; now's the time to assess them against the program's goals.

If your race is lagging, it's time to take a pit stop and make adjustments. A security company, for example, was introducing three shifts and wanted to offer first choice of shifts to its top call center performers, defined as those who handled the most calls. Guess what? Anyone can handle lots of calls if they hang up prematurely on one customer to take the next one. Uh-oh. It was time for a pit stop.

As that story illustrates, it isn't only speed that matters. It's precision. You want to make sure you're staying on course, listening to feedback, running the race efficiently. You want to make sure you have the energy to finish the race.

If you're getting amazing results, you will be tempted to extend the race (see Chapter 4). But trust me, that is a bad idea. People will lose the sense of urgency. Soon they'll be taking a road trip instead of competing in the Indy.

> **Long story short: Take a pit stop to make adjustments.** A major telecommunications firm wanted its sales reps to validate new sales-skill knowledge within 15 days. Five days into this time period, only 2% of the reps had taken the quiz.
>
> The company's leaders wanted to—you guessed it—double the reward for taking the quiz. Wrong consequence! That would encourage reps to hold out longer next time for an even larger reward.
>
> So instead, leaders decided to reward managers who had 90% of their reps take the knowledge quiz within the next two weeks. The Call to Action behaviors for managers: Review the audiotape training with reps and help reps apply the quiz information to their next five appointments.
>
> After this mid-course adjustment, the program's goal was met several times over. The results showed a huge increase in first-contact meetings with customers.

Never a Dull Moment

The key thing to remember about metrics is that you have to look at them in a way you've never looked at them before. Calls are getting longer? Why? It may take some pondering to figure it out. And it may not be the number crunchers who can figure it out. Get creative people with lots of common sense working on the problem. (Sorry, number crunchers.)

Look at the results goal in your Call to Action: sales closed, commitments made (accounts receivable), issues resolved (call centers). Who's doing it best? Why?

Don't yawn. It really does not have to be tedious. You designed the program around certain metrics in the first place. If those numbers have changed, figure out why. Use what you have to run the best race possible.

When you see the checkered flag, get ready to celebrate. Then take a break and get your green flag ready. It won't be long 'til the next race!

10

WHAT TO DO NEXT

As I promised out of the gate, I've shown you how to focus people's behaviors on what is really important. Since you've gotten this far in the book, I'll give you a B.S. in behavior-based rewards. But until you've *applied* the information you've learned, its value isn't worth much more than those two letters on your degree.

So the question is this: Have you focused your *own* behavior on what's really important? What are the two behaviors and one result you must accomplish to accelerate your company's growth NOW? How about something like this:

Call to Action – You
- **Magic-wand Wish:** To increase sales/profit/revenue for my organization this quarter.
- **Behavior (Knowledge):** Finish reading this chapter to reinforce the principles for building a behavior-based reward program.
- **Behavior:** Find a partner who understands behavior-based rewards.
- **Result:** Put a program in place by one month from today for accelerating growth in my organization by xx%. (You fill in the goal. It should have double digits.)

Remember, talk is cheap. If you aren't going to use what you've read, you've just been wasting your time.

Here's a quick review of the principles for creating a behavior-based reward program:

{*Principle 1.*} **Start with what you have and keep it simple.** Define your Call to Action in terms of two behaviors and one result. Post the signs in the maze so people know they're going the right direction.

{*Principle 2.*} **Dramatize your Call to Action.** Throw a party to introduce the goals and consequences of the program. Keep communicating the Call to Action in a variety of ways.

{*Principle 3.*} **Play the game just long enough to win.** Run your program no longer than 60 days past the time it takes to achieve the behavior. Get others to copy the behaviors of your top performers to accelerate results. Celebrate in the end zone. Then raise the bar slightly when you introduce your next Call to Action.

{*Principle 4.*} **Maximize the mix: cash, recognition and rewards.** Don't use compensation (eg., higher commissions) as a reward. If you reward with cash in any form, later, when you take that cash away, it'll feel like a cut in pay. For optimum performance, mix what people are already getting in base pay and commission, with rewards and recognition.

{*Principle 5.*} **Get the most for your money.** Don't pay for results you would've gotten anyway. Find out what your top performers are doing to increase revenue and profits. Reward everyone else for copying the top performers. Project program ROI and remember to recycle the byproducts of the program—hidden savings many companies overlook.

{*Principle 6.*} **Make sure your rewards are rewarding.** Give employees a selection of non-cash rewards, and let them dream about their goal while they're working to earn it. Catch participants doing things right and recognize them with *e*Points. Don't forget to mix team and individual rewards.

{*Principle 7.*} **Check your focus.** Double-check the program's goals against your strategy. Make sure managers are willing to reinforce the Call to Action behaviors. Check the program for fairness. Check the Call to Action for verifiability. Keep checking along the way to make sure you're on course and everyone's playing. Get ready to celebrate a smooth landing.

{*Principle 8.*} **Watch your gauges and make adjustments.** If you're attentive, you'll find the hidden stories in your program's measurements. Watch who gets involved, who's doing it best and why, and what improvements you're getting over the last program. Take pit stops to make adjustments at strategic times.

Now let's talk about the second behavior in your Call to Action: Find a partner who understands behavior-based rewards. **If there's one thing you can't afford, it's a partner who's a loser!**

Find a Partner Who Understands Behavior-Based Rewards

You're probably thinking: We can do this. We have people in marketing who can communicate the Call to Action. We have meeting planners who can throw a party. Purchasing can fulfill the rewards and accounting can track the costs. Our travel agency can plan trips for the top performers. No problem.

Please listen to the voice of experience. Don't try this on your own. You will spend countless hours—and resources—figuring out that it isn't as easy as it may appear. Your high-performance racecar, once it's built, may end up looking more like a low-tech go-cart.

Sure, you say, this is just Louise's ploy to get more business. Well, I wouldn't mind having more business, but my company may or may not be a good fit for your company. So here are a few questions you'll want to ask when you're looking for a rewarding partner:

What's the company's core business? Before you engage a firm, look at its core business. If it mainly sells trinkets, move on. If it's into marketing, advertising, management consulting, training or merchandise fulfillment, look elsewhere. That company will not be able to provide what you need in terms of a comprehensive behavior-change program. If you're looking at a company whose core business is performance improvement, you're ready for the next step.

Does the candidate reward for behaviors? Sales made, money committed, calls completed. These are good things. But how do you get there? If your prospective partner can't help you define some early indicators in the form of behaviors, find someone who can.

What is the recommended Call to Action? If people accomplish that Call to Action, will they achieve your key corporate strategies? If not, make another call.

Does your potential partner understand how to clone the behaviors of top performers? This is the key strategy for moving the performance curve forward—that is, expanding your repertoire of top performers. Your partner should be able to coach your managers to coach each other.

Is your potential partner recommending cash or non-cash rewards? If they argue too hard for cash, be very, very suspicious. Somebody may be taking the lazy way out.

Can the company design an *e*Points system? An *e*Points system is more than just Web-based reports; it's a sophisticated banking system. This should be no problem for a performance improvement company.

Can the firm produce online and print communications? It's important to coordinate program communications so that participants aren't confused by conflicting messages and designs. Communications should fit the corporate culture and should be attractive and high quality without requiring a high-end budget.

Can the company verify the program's results and track tax liability? How will you know:
- When you've hit your projected numbers?
- When you've achieved ROI that more than covers the cost of the program?

If the company can't measure the results of the program, find a partner who can.

Get Results NOW!

In closing, here's some personal advice straight from my heart: **Don't wait to take action on these ideas!** I've learned from hard experience that once I decide something is right, I need to move on it—especially when the cost of doing nothing far outweighs the potential expense of the new venture. What do I have to lose?

If you're planning to sit there, on the same part of your anatomy you were sitting on when you first picked up this book, I have one question: **What are you waiting for?**

Your cream of the corp. is ready to rise to the top! This book has demonstrated that your company's best ideas are just waiting to be tapped, and that you don't have to be a rocket scientist to do it.

You wouldn't believe how many leaders—even though they know that **doing nothing** is costing them millions every month!—are still not ready to call their people to action. For most, I've discovered that what it takes is a sign from above, in the form of a kick in the behind. Does top management have to put *your* backside on the chopping block before you're willing to take action?

While your boss is busy analyzing the autopsy numbers—incremental margin gained (or lost, as the case may be)—your company's top performers and the undiscovered leaders in your Eighty Percent Club are doing what it takes to produce results. Your job is to figure out what they're doing that works and then show *everyone* how to copy the successful behaviors.

If you don't do it *now,* you're risking that you'll lose just as much this month as you did last month. You're risking that your best performers will take their ideas and go use them for your competitors. You're risking that *you* won't have a job after next quarter's results are posted.

Where do you start? Get going on your personal Call to Action. Review the principles. Find a partner who can help you build a behavior-based program. Then call your people to action. It shouldn't take you more than 30 days to start seeing results.

If you have the courage to take this challenge, I want to hear from you. E-mail me at lsanderson@andersonperformance.com and share your results. I expect to hear that your people are accelerating profits—double-digit profits—NOW!